WITHDRAWN

GOOD GUILT, BAD GUILT

And What To Do With Each

BECCA COWAN JOHNSON

InterVarsity Press
Downers Grove, Illinois

InterVarsity Press® is the book-publishing division of InterVarsity Christian Fellowship®, a student movement active on campus at hundreds of universities, colleges and schools of nursing in the United States of America, and a member movement of the International Fellowship of Evangelical Students. For information about local and regional activities, write Public Relations Dept., InterVarsity Christian Fellowship, 6400 Schroeder Rd., P.O. Box 7895, Madison, WI 53707-7895.

All Scripture quotations, unless otherwise indicated, are taken from the HOLY BIBLE, NEW INTERNATIONAL VERSION®. NIV®. Copyright © 1973, 1978, 1984 by International Bible Society. Used by permission of Zondervan Publishing House. All rights reserved.

Excerpt in chapter one is reprinted from A Do-It-at-Home Retreat: The Spiritual Exercises of St. Ignatius Loyola, by André Ravier, pp. 231 © 1989 Ignatius Press, San Francisco. All rights reserved; reprinted with permission of Ignatius Press.

ISBN 0-8308-1956-8

Printed in the United States of America ∞

Library of Congress Cataloging-in-Publication Data

Johnson, Becca Cowan, 1954-
    Good guilt, bad guilt: and what to do with each/ Becca Cowan
Johnson.
      p.   cm.
    Includes bibliographical references.
    ISBN 0-8308-1956-8 (pbk.: alk. paper)
    1. Guilt—Religious aspects—Christianity. 2. Guilt—
Psychological aspects—Christianity. 3. Satisfaction—Religious
aspects—Christianity. 4. Forgiveness—Religious aspects—
Christianity. I. Title.
BJ1471.5.J64   1996
233'.4—dc20   95-26746
                                    CIP

16	15	14	13	12	11	10	9	8	7	6	5	4	3	2	1
09	08	07	06	05	04	03	02	01	00	99	98	97	96		

To my wonderful family;
To the many people who struggle with guilt
over big and little things;
And to the One who frees us from guilt.

Acknowledgments

I am especially thankful to Don Richmond for his encouragement, thought-provoking ideas, writings, resources and critique. His theological and psychological input were invaluable. Susie Colby and Wynnae Huizinga Bliss provided wonderful assistance in evaluating both the content and writing style of the book. I am also grateful for the helpful and challenging theological insights and recommendations given by pastors Chip Ingram and Lane Webster.

I also want to thank those who critiqued all or part of this book while it was in process. They helped mold the shape of the manuscript with their comments and suggestions. Thank you to Peter Holdaas, Karen Mitchell, Jayne Price, Avis Cowan, Krista Barlow, Nancy Scambler, Patty Regalia and Susan Waller.

To the many people who have shared their concerns and struggles with me over the years, I am grateful and honored. I have grown both personally and professionally because of you. Thank you also to the many people who completed the guilt surveys I developed or told me their personal stories of guilt.

My wonderful family showed me much encouragement and support, not to mention patience, during the development of this book. Thank you, Lloyd, Krista, Jordan and Katie.

O N E

Why Examine Guilt?

*W*hile growing up as the only child of a single parent, Sam was continually told, "You must take care of me; you're all I've got." Whenever he disobeyed, his mother responded, "You must make Mommy happy. Only you can make Mommy happy." These beliefs placed an enormous burden on Sam's little shoulders. When he grew up, his big shoulders still bore the burden of his mother's well-being. Every time his mother expressed disapproval, disappointment or dejection, he felt responsible. Though guilt surrounded him on all sides, he didn't recognize it. To him, his feelings were the result of his failure.

Through counseling, Sam began to identify and face his own feelings of guilt regarding his mother. He came to understand that he had tried to give his guilt feelings away to his wife. Once his wife stopped accepting his guilt, he had to deal with it once again. When he finally faced it, he realized that he wasn't responsible for his mother's happiness. What he was feeling was unnecessary guilt—bad guilt.

If you and I were to walk down the street and come upon a man pointing at us from a soapbox pedestal and shouting, "Guilty! Guilty!

Guilty!" neither of us could argue with the accusation. As fallen human beings we are all too capable of committing errors in judgment, action and thought. Guilt is no stranger to us. As one person lamented, "I feel guilt whenever I make a mistake, forget something, lose something, get somewhere a minute late or see that my windows are dirty."

We all experience guilt to varying degrees, whether we realize it or not. Some of us are constantly plagued with feelings of guilt, while others of us experience it less often. If you have ever tried to eliminate guilt from your life, you've discovered that it's an impossible task. Tricia wrote, "I feel guilty when my parents feel neglected, when my spouse is angry, when my children don't obey and when things aren't going well at work." She jokingly added, "Other than that, I don't experience guilt too much!"

In my work as a psychologist, I encounter numerous people burdened by guilt due to an affair, an abortion, an accident or an addiction. Some have struggled with lust, masturbation, pornography, alcohol, drugs, eating disorders, hatred or being a sexually active Christian single. Others have felt guilty whenever their parents fought, when a sibling died or when they were sexually abused. Many others expressed guilt for feeling angry, being overweight, watching "inappropriate" movies, not living up to their parents' expectations, not being more successful, not praying more, not getting better grades or not flossing their teeth regularly. *Whether the guilt-producer is big or small, deserved or undeserved, actual or perceived, most of us feel guilty in one way or another.*

The more I work with those affected by guilt, the more I realize its pervasiveness. At first I thought that only certain types of people were affected by guilt's negative influence. Then I began to see that almost everyone who sought counseling had roots of guilt growing somewhere in their emotional garden. I was amazed to discover how much guilt feelings permeate and even motivate our lives.

That's right—*our* lives. As I have examined many of my own thoughts, actions and feelings, I've come to realize that guilt has been an ever-present part of my life. If I forget to return a phone call, I feel guilty. When I throw away financial pleas from charitable organizations, some twinges of guilt come along. When I don't get around to doing things (writing to friends, spending time with the kids, cleaning the house), guilt pays a visit. The list goes on and on, with big as well as little areas of guilt. I have yet to go a day without feeling guilt to some degree or another.

I also realized that my guilt feelings affect my relationship with God. When I neglect to spend time in prayer and reading the Bible, guilt begins to grow. It gains momentum and size like a snowball rolling down a slope until I find myself hesitating to go to God at all. My prayers soon become filled with apologies rather than adoration, with petitions for pardon rather than praise. A pastor once asked, "If God loves us so much, why do we experience it so little?" He went on to say, "Guilt gets in the way." *God never intended us to be motivated by guilt.*

Guilt is not something we readily recognize. Many of us experience an unending barrage of guilt feelings without even knowing it. We may have become so accustomed to guilt's presence that we are unaware of its effect on our attitudes and actions. It's like a hidden virus in our thoughts and feelings.

If we *are* aware of constant guilt feelings, we may become either too overwhelmed to do anything about them or too embarrassed to share our inner burden. Feeling weak, insecure and vulnerable, we don't want others to know of our guilty convictions. We may incorrectly assume that we are the only ones attacked by the constant inner cry, "Guilty!"

In C. S. Lewis's delightful and entertaining book *The Screwtape Letters*, he depicts the duties of a hardworking demon assigned to a man who has become a Christian. The demon's job is to cause the man to stumble in his Christian endeavors. In the story we discover that one of the enemy's favorite tactics is to encourage the human to dwell on his inadequacies, because they inevitably lead him to feel guilty.[1]

In the Bible, Satan is referred to as the "accuser" and the "father of lies" (Rev 12:10; Jn 8:44). He hurls accusations and lies at us because he knows that they lead us to feel guilty. Guilt is one of his most powerful tools for getting us to focus on ourselves and our perceived and real inadequacies rather than on God's love, mercy and forgiveness.

Do You Feel Guilty?
Here are some of the many areas in which we may feel guilty. With which do you identify?

Do you feel guilty about . . .

☐ what you should or shouldn't eat?

☐ your lack of time management skills?

☐ not knowing what's going on in the world?

☐ your long-forgotten New Year's resolutions?

☐ your parenting skills?

☐ not keeping in touch with friends and family?

☐ your job?

☐ your home not being as clean as your mother-in-law's?

☐ not doing everything the doctor tells you to do?

☐ making a wrong decision?

☐ asking the waitress to take back your uncooked burger?

☐ not having perfect, obedient children?

☐ forgetting to call your mother?

☐ not having the perfect body?

☐ not giving more money to charitable causes?

☐ passing a lonely hitchhiker?

☐ not giving (or giving in and giving) to a beggar?

☐ feeling angry or jealous?

☐ unwanted habits (like smoking, nail-biting)?

☐ not spending more time in prayer or Bible study?

☐ not exercising enough?

☐ watching too much TV?

☐ doing anything for yourself, because you feel selfish?

☐ not being able to please everyone, even yourself?

☐ not being a perfect person, patient parent, exemplary employee and/or fabulous friend?

And do you feel guilty because . . .

☐ you don't "like" one of your children?

☐ you had an abortion or gave a baby up for adoption?

☐ you're having an affair?

☐ one of your children died (whether an accident or a suicide) or is disabled?

☐ you lost your temper and hit one of your children?

☐ you wish something terrible would happen to your domineering parent?

☐ you've been sexually active as a single?

☐ you embezzled money or stole equipment from your workplace?

☐ you continue to struggle with an addiction?

☐ you were driving and had an accident in which someone was killed or badly injured?

☐ you don't "love" your spouse?

☐ you lie?

☐ you're a compulsive gambler?

☐ you struggle with lust, masturbation, pornography and/or fantasizing?

☐ you did something foolish that changed the course of your life?

☐ you've attempted suicide?

☐ you question God's existence and love?

There are plenty of big and little, significant and insignificant things to feel guilty about. It seems that no one is immune to guilt.

Dealing with Guilt

When we experience guilt, we often deal with it in ways that are unhealthy and counterproductive. This is illustrated well in the first biblical account of guilt in Genesis 3:1-13. The serpent convinces Eve to partake of the forbidden fruit. Eve then gives it to Adam to eat. In verses 7-12 we read,

> Then the eyes of both of them were opened, and they realized they were naked . . . and they hid from the LORD God among the trees of the garden. But the LORD God called to the man, "Where are you?" He answered, "I heard you in the garden, and I was afraid

because I was naked; so I hid." And he said, "Who told you that you were naked? Have you eaten from the tree that I commanded you not to eat from?" The man said, "The woman you put here with me—she gave me some fruit from the tree, and I ate it." Then the LORD God said to the woman, "What is this you have done?" The woman said, "The serpent deceived me, and I ate."

In this account of the Fall we can identify numerous ill-adaptive ways of dealing with guilt. When confronted with their actual guilt of disobedience, Adam and Eve employed and experienced a variety of unhealthy responses. *Their guilt led them to hide, to avoid individual responsibility, to feel self-conscious, to withdraw from God, to feel vulnerable, to bring others down, to deny wrongdoing, to fear others' opinions, to feel shame, to develop a victim mentality and to project blame.*

Like Adam and Eve, we use ineffective techniques in dealing with guilt. Keith Krull, a Christian psychologist, refers to these as the symptoms of guilt and states, "The Bible starts by giving us a detailed description of guilt. Apparently God felt it important that we understand it early on. Yet it remains very misunderstood in Christian circles and has caused enormous problems psychologically and spiritually for centuries."[2]

The Harmful Effects of Guilt

British statesman and political writer Edmund Burke addressed the topic of guilt when he spoke before the House of Commons: "Guilt was never a rational thing; it distorts all the faculties of the human mind, it perverts them, it leaves a man no longer in the free use of his reason, it puts him into confusion." Though these words were spoken over two hundred years ago, they still ring true today. The effects and nature of guilt do not change—guilt can cause us to become irrational and our thinking to become distorted, perverted and confused.

Guilt's negative effects spread to all parts of our lives: spiritual, emotional, mental, physical and social. We may feel alienated from God, fearing his judgment and wrath. As we sense our guilt or sin, we develop a self-imposed separation from him. We may feel overcome with self-condemnation or denial. We may begin to feel depressed, anxious or angry. We may also find it more difficult to concentrate and to feel productive when our mind dwells on guilt. We forget obligations, become easily distracted, seem unfocused and misplace things more readily. As we experience the effects of stress-producing guilt our body's resistance may also weaken. We develop headaches, ulcers, tense muscles or cold sores, and we become more susceptible to heart attacks and other stress-related physical problems.

Our relationships with friends and family also suffer as a result of our guilt burden. One man begins to express anger at his wife because he feels guilty for having to work long hours and be away from the family. One woman begins avoiding a friend at work when she feels guilty for having been promoted over her. If we avoid facing our guilt feelings, we often also avoid facing those around us. Our relationships suffer when guilt lurks within us.

Once we let guilt into our hearts and minds and let it control our feelings and thoughts, we fall prey to its powerful influence. Psychologist and family advocate James Dobson writes,

Few human emotions are as distressing and painful as feelings of guilt and personal disapproval. When at a peak of intensity, self-condemnation gnaws on the conscious mind by day and invades the dreams by night. Since the voice of the conscience speaks from inside the human mind, we cannot escape its unrelenting abuse for our mistakes, failures and sins. For some particularly vulnerable individuals, an internal taskmaster is on the job from early morning until late at night—screaming accusations at his tormented victim.[3]

Our task is to silence the screaming accusations of the internal taskmaster. We do this by ridding ourselves of unnecessary guilt. When we do this, we regain control over our thoughts, feelings and actions so that inappropriate guilt no longer reigns over us. Burdens are lifted, hopes restored and fears diminished. We need to be like a reptile that yearly sheds its outer layer of skin as part of its growing process.

As we shed the burden of guilt, we are free to grow. Negative feelings of inadequacy are replaced by a more realistic sense of self. Spiritually, we move from a shameful stance before God to embracing our position as beloved children. We are better able to concentrate on tasks at hand, free of constant reminders of failures. We have more energy and are less susceptible to stress, illness, aches and pains. We are more willing to face others once we have faced our unwanted and awkward feelings.

Understanding the bad aspects of guilt frees us to face the good aspects of it. As we acknowledge our sin and sinful nature, we remove the barriers we had erected between us and our Creator. *Accepting our true guilt and ignoring bad guilt increases our ability to experience God's amazing grace, mercy, forgiveness and love.*

Guilt Prone or Guilt Projectors?

Many of us fall into two categories when it comes to guilt. Some are more sensitive and overwhelmed by it (guilt prone), while others are more numb to it or readily pass it on to others (guilt projectors).

Donnie, a young married woman, frequently says, "I'm sorry." She assumes it's her fault whenever something goes wrong. "I'm sorry" is said without much thought or meaning, but with much guilt. Those words have become so common that she doesn't realize how often she utters them.

Kevin was attending a staff meeting and noticed that Beth wasn't there. Later he said, "I caught myself thinking that it was my fault she wasn't there. Maybe I should have called and reminded her. Maybe I should have offered her a ride. Maybe I should have asked to have the meeting rescheduled."

Guilt-prone people act as magnets for guilt. They are quick to assume guilt for any misunderstanding, disagreement, awkward situation or inappropriate action. They live by an unspoken motto that they are guilty unless proven undeniably innocent. Even when evidence does prove their innocence, they might assume the facts (and themselves) to be faulty. One person summed it up: "Some people claim more guilt than they actually earned. That's meaningless pain—and that's crazy."

Robbie is also in this category. "I wrote a letter to my friend and even made a long-distance call, leaving a message on her answering machine. Several weeks went by and she didn't respond. I began to assume that I must have done something to offend her. I started thinking back to see if I could find any remote, possible cause for her to be mad at me. Even though I couldn't find one, I still assumed I must have done something wrong. I decided that the fact that I couldn't find the reason didn't mean a reason didn't exist; it meant that my detective skills were unable to uncover my blunder. The thought hadn't occurred to me that her lack of correspondence could possibly be anything other than my fault."

Robbie went on, "When my friend finally contacted me, she apologized profusely, stating that she had been feeling guilty for letting so much time go by. She'd felt so guilty that it almost prevented her from ever getting back in contact with me. Her guilt and my guilt could have danced all night!"

What increases our sensitivity to guilt? Self-doubt, feelings of shame, emotional sensitivity, an overactive conscience, immaturity of faith, lack of knowledge of God's Word, legalism, distorted views of God, sinful deeds and thoughts, among others.

Those with guilt-prone personalities attract guilt like a light bulb attracts bugs and are easy targets for those who project their blame and guilt onto others. Those in this latter group, the guilt projectors, seem not to be bothered by unrelenting and undeserved guilt feelings. They block their feelings and live a numbed existence. If they do experience guilt, they become quite good at finding the guilt prone, who readily accept guilt without question.

It seems, then, that we are either overly sensitive to guilt or detached from it. Either way, the enemy of our souls wins a victory. This is well addressed in André Ravier's book on the *Spiritual Exercises* of St. Ignatius Loyola:

Satan keeps a watchful eye on the soul, determining if it is blunted or sensitive. If sensitive, he works to the point of making it excessively refined so that he can more easily trouble it and upset it. For example, if he sees that the soul does not consent to committing either a mortal or a venial sin, nor does it entertain anything that even appears to be deliberately sinful, he tries to make it imagine sins where there are none present—for example, in some word or thought that has absolutely no importance whatsoever.

Does Satan busy himself in the opposite way with a blunted mind? Here he attempts to make the soul even more blunted. For example, if the soul pays no attention to venial sins, he will encourage it to pay little heed to mortal sins. If before it had some fear of a mortal sin, he will try to minimize or even do away altogether with such fear.

The soul that desires to make progress in the spiritual life ought always to take the opposite course to that proposed by Satan. If he seeks to make the soul more blunted, it should apply itself to making itself more sensitive. If he tries to supersensitize the soul, it must force itself to become tougher so as to establish itself between these extremes, where it can enjoy perfect peace.[4]

What makes us overly sensitive or overly blunted? Many factors contribute to how we respond (or don't respond) to guilt. Some of us have *personalities* which are sensitive and emotional by nature. We respond to situations with tenderness and an acute awareness of feelings. Others of us are more logical, rational and mentally (not emotionally) oriented. Also our *self-perspective* may be full of self-hatred, shame, self-doubt and disgust, which makes us more vulnerable to guilt. Or perhaps our *past*, with a variety of negative experiences, has programmed us to automatically accept or reject guilt. One of our goals, then, is to sensitize the numbed soul and to desensitize the overly sensitive one.

Where Do We Go from Here?

This book is for all of us. It is for those of us seeking forgiveness from the guilt of our sins (good guilt) *and* for those of us seeking relief from needless guilt (bad guilt). It is for those overly sensitive to guilt, those insensitive to it and all those in between. The information here will help us minimize the harmful effects of bad guilt and maximize the benefits of good guilt. In order to do this we must identify sources of guilt as well as our counterproductive attempts to deal with guilt.

We will examine what guilt is and how it develops. We will take a look at some of the many sources of guilt in our lives—those people, places and things that trigger our guilt feelings. We will explore the ways guilt hides within our actions and attitudes. We will dissect guilt so that we better understand the components that are helpful and those that are harmful. We will seek to better understand God's perspective on guilt and the role of conviction, confession and forgiveness. We will learn what steps to take in minimizing bad guilt and what to do with good guilt.

The information in these pages comes from personal and professional experience as well as from various sources (books, journals, articles, presentations). Helpful information was also gathered from several surveys I developed on guilt. The respondents were asked to identify areas in which they felt guilty and the frequency of their guilt feelings, and to share any advice for distinguishing between good and bad guilt and getting rid of unnecessary guilt. They provided insight into the many specific ways we experience guilt. Those who completed the surveys were pastors and laypersons, counselors and clients, women and men, young and old.

Here's where we're going. Here's our Guilt Game Plan.

Guilt Game Plan

Recognize	the existence and prevalence of guilt
Identify	the sources of guilt
Acknowledge	our ineffective ways of dealing with guilt
Face	guilt and guilty feelings
Distinguish	between good and bad guilt
Eliminate	bad guilt
Respond	to good guilt

Our goal is to be free of bad guilt and to respond appropriately to good guilt. This endeavor will help us more fully experience God's grace, mercy, love, forgiveness, joy, freedom and peace.

Application Questions
1. In what areas do you generally feel guilty?
2. In addition, which of the items listed under "Do you feel guilty about . . ." or "Do you feel guilty because . . ." do you experience as guilt-producing?
3. When Adam and Eve's guilt was exposed, their responses demonstrated some of the ineffective ways we deal with guilt. How do you respond when your guilt is exposed?

Prayer
Lord, help us to be sensitive to the Holy Spirit and not overly sensitive or overly blunted to guilt. Amen.

TWO

Good Versus Bad Guilt

*M*argery and Bart came in for marriage counseling after he had confessed to having an affair. He felt ashamed and guilty. So did she. As they expressed their feelings about their relationship, it became apparent that Margery's feelings of guilt were not well founded. "I feel like his affair is my fault," she said. "I feel so guilty. I should be a better wife." Bart, on the other hand, felt guilty for lying to his wife and being unfaithful.

Margery needed to let go of her undeserved guilt and deal with her feelings of inadequacy. Bart needed to let his guilt lead him to repentance and draw him closer to our forgiving, loving God. They both felt remorse. They both felt guilty. One was experiencing bad guilt, the other good guilt.

A popular perspective currently gaining momentum tells us to get rid of guilt altogether. Guilt is seen as harmful, not helpful; useless, not useful. The secular counselor's perspective lumps all guilt together and advises us to avoid, ignore or annihilate it. This view, however, is bound to throw society into a tailspin. In the *Journal of Ethics*

Herbert Morris warns, "Much is lost in any world . . . pulled . . . away from guilt, because [when] we flee our anxiety, we shall end up facing a monster more fearful than the one from which we have fled."[1] Ignoring guilt doesn't make it go away. Instead, it may grow more hideous and overwhelming than it originally was.

Society is right when it encourages us to shed excess guilt. However, *not all guilt is bad—some guilt is good for us.* Guilt can encourage or discourage us, challenge or condemn us. What we need to do is learn how to separate the good from the bad.

Rabbi Harlan Wechsler writes about good and bad guilt. "We live in times when the distinction between the two is commonly blurred in people's minds. It is important to know when guilt is a help and when it is a hindrance. For it can be both. We need to remember guilt's duality in order to engage it head-on. Otherwise guilt is just an incomprehensible enemy, always lying in wait to attack."[2]

But how can we distinguish between good guilt and bad guilt? How can we get rid of illegitimate, destructive guilt and glean the rewards of true, beneficial guilt?

The Difference Between Good Guilt and Bad Guilt

Good guilt teaches us where we have erred and thus where we need to change. Good guilt is that which we *should* feel—the appropriate response when we have sinned. Rather than wallow in our sin, we allow the guilt produced by our trespass to challenge and change us in ways that glorify God. Authentic guilt motivates, prods and pushes us to be all that God intended us to be. *Good guilt draws us closer to God as we turn to him for forgiveness.*

We can think of good guilt as being true, legitimate, healthy, real, motivating, constructive, objective, authentic or actual guilt. It is helpful, necessary guilt. As one person said, "It's good to feel guilty when you are."

In contrast, bad guilt reminds us of our shortcomings and undermines our spiritual growth. It leads to despair, discouragement, depression and disappointment. Bad guilt immobilizes us when we should be moving forward. It can hinder our development, stunt our growth and restrict our freedom. Mindy wrote, "Guilt keeps me stuck. I sometimes feel so guilty about not completing a task that I guarantee it doesn't get finished."

Bad guilt keeps us in a pit of mud and mire when God desires to place our feet on a rock and give us a firm place to stand (Ps 40:2). It weighs us down and keep us from becoming the people God desires us to be. "This guilt is one of the major causes of spiritual deadness and defeat."[3] Even our unhealthy responses to true guilt can turn a good thing into a bad thing. Dan described it well: "Guilt is the always hungry lion! It is something that eats a person alive internally." Bad guilt can destroy and defeat our attempts at being all that we can be. *Bad guilt distracts us from God because we focus on ourselves and not him.*

We can think of bad guilt as being false, illegitimate, psychological, binding, unhealthy, perceived, corrosive, unproductive, incapacitating, imaginary, destructive, subjective, unnecessary or inappropriate guilt.

Unfortunately, *bad guilt is not easily recognized.* It is sly, subversive and subtle. It often works undercover, wearing various masks and disguises. Those who are able to identify and face good guilt are transformed by it. Those who are overwhelmed by bad guilt are tyrannized by it.

Some refer to bad guilt as psychological, neurotic or pathological guilt and shame. True or good guilt has been referred to as actual guilt and godly or constructive sorrow (2 Cor 7:9-10).

Why We Hold on to Bad Guilt

Before we can begin the process of distinguishing between good and bad guilt, we must acknowledge that some of us actually prefer keeping guilt around. We may be hesitant to rid ourselves of guilt because we've discovered (consciously or subconsciously) some of the advantages to having it stay. That is, we've learned how to use it on our behalf. These "benefits" must be exposed as impostors that actually keep us from approaching guilt as God desires.

We divert the real issues. When we focus on guilt rather than the root of the guilt, we create a diversion from the real issues. We direct our attention to the guilt and neglect dealing with why we experienced it in the first place. We are clever in our coverups and sly in our shroud—guilt keeps us from facing the core issues. "False guilt when probed is always a door to what are our real issues."[4]

We manipulate and control. A destructive effect of being fraught with guilt is that we can use it to control and manipulate others. People are less likely to confront or challenge us if we are overcome with guilt. They also won't expect much from us. So whenever we sense an uncomfortable situation, we turn on our guilt-ridden demeanor and control conversations, relationships and others' expectations.

As we dwell in this sorrowful state we build a wall around us, hoping that no one will get in. The wall gets higher and stronger as we see its effectiveness in keeping others at a distance.

We get attention. If we display our guilt enough, we will surely grab the attention of others who want to help us in our despair. We will take center stage in conversations and relationships—the focus will be on us. Others' energies will be spent trying to help us and encourage us. Judith Viorst humorously wrote, "My friend, Louise, feels guilty about wanting to be admired for feeling guilty."[5] Even though they may feel guilty about it, some want to be admired for feeling guilty because they love the attention.

We receive pity. Guilt can also be used to elicit pity from others. We share our woes in order to gain sympathy. We want warmth and understanding rather than the condemnation we feel we deserve. Those who pity us are less likely to confront or challenge us.

We attract others. Guilt can be helpful when we lack social skills and feel awkward in developing and sustaining relationships. Sharing our feelings and struggles helps us to connect with others. As we wallow in our guilt, we attract others, generally those who need to be needed or to feel superior. As a result our relationships are unhealthy and one-sided and lack mutuality.

We avoid failure and success. Sometimes we use guilt to disguise our fears. Rather than face those things that keep us from moving ahead, we retreat into guilt. If we fear failure, we use guilt as our excuse for not attempting new things. We give up even before trying.

One author cited fear of success as another way we use guilt to our advantage. "Guilt may also be used by the person who fears success. Most guilt-ridden persons know how to fail but they don't know how to succeed. . . . [They use guilt as] 'smokescreens' to avoid new attempts that might lead to success."[6]

We feel more in control. Many of us may find guilt a more comfortable emotion than anger, jealousy, envy or hatred. We express
feelings of guilt while repressing these other less desirable emotions.
Why? Because we fear our anger and what we might do or say, and
we despise our jealousy. We'd rather deal with our feelings of guilt
about not being able to love someone than deal with our feelings of
hate toward them. We bury such unwanted feelings beneath the sod
of guilt, all in an attempt to avoid the deeper issues.

We avoid change. Not only is guilt a more comfortable and control-
lable emotion, but for many of us it has also become familiar. It's a
part of who we are and how we view ourselves, God, others and our
world. Guilt is a housemate, a long-time companion. We fear the
emotions, fears and hurts that might jump into its place if it were
ousted.

One person said, "When I realized I didn't have to feel guilty all the
time I was really frightened because I didn't know how to feel. Even
though I didn't like the old feelings, I was used to them. I had to start
all over and that was scary."

We avoid others' scrutiny. The authors of *Cry of the Soul* write,
"Guilt is . . . a perversely self-centered effort to escape the wound and
the potential for judgment."[7] When we demonstrate remorse, we insulate ourselves from external examination. If others see that we are
already penitent for our wrongdoings, they are less likely to confront
us with their concerns. We use a sorrowful façade to elude further
disapproval.

The Good and the Bad
Guilt can be bad, and the ways we use it can also be bad for us. God
desires that we deal with guilt in ways that honor him. He also desires
that we learn to separate the good from the bad. We are to disregard
false guilt and turn to him with our true guilt. The distinction between
good guilt and bad guilt is not always clear, however. It is not simply
a matter of separating sheep from goats. The following chapters will
help us understand guilt and its origins.

Application Questions
1. In what ways does society encourage us to get rid of all guilt?

2. What does the Bible say about guilt? What are some biblical examples of good and bad guilt?
3. Do you use guilt to your advantage? In what ways?

Prayer
Lord, we desire to be able to distinguish between good and bad guilt so that we may not be distracted from knowing your heart. Help us to let go of guilt so that we can hold on to you. Thank you. Amen.

THREE

Understanding Guilt

Since Sandra became a Christian, she has found herself feeling more and more guilty. "Before I was a Christian I didn't feel so bad. Now I feel like the ball in a pinball machine, getting hit and bounced around from one guilt to another. The more I learn about believing in God, the more I feel guilty. The more I read my Bible or go to church, the more I feel guilty. I feel guilty about a lot of things a lot of the time." Sandra needs to understand both God and guilt better.

When it comes to guilt we are wise to follow the advice of Anatole France, who said, "It is better to understand a little than to misunderstand a lot." Understanding the nature, emergence and complexities of guilt is not an easy task. Volumes have been written on the subject. We must satisfy ourselves with a quick overview, lest we be overwhelmed and caught up in century-long debates. Let's try to understand at least a little so that we don't misunderstand a lot.

What Is Guilt?
In simple terms, guilt could be defined as a wrong committed, but that

inadequately conveys the complexity of guilt. Guilt is often confused with condemnation, embarrassment, humiliation, regret, remorse, repentance, blame and shame. While it may involve these terms, it isn't accurately described by them.

Guilt has been defined as "an emotional response to the perception that we have broken a prohibition or have fallen short of a standard."[1] According to this definition, guilt can be emotional rather than logical and can be based on perception rather than reality.

Guilt may be based on shifting or absolute values, on an actual transgression or a perceived indiscretion. What determines right and wrong may seem clear in one era and elusive and confusing in another. Things considered sinful in the past are now readily accepted in the Christian community (such as playing cards, wearing high heels, going to movies). From culture to culture and from decade to decade, what causes guilt can both change and remain the same.

Guilt and Guilt Feelings
The complexity of guilt is increased when we realize that it can be both a fact and a feeling, and that the two aren't necessarily related. We may be guilty of wrongdoing yet not feel guilty, as might be the case with a psychopath (antisocial personality disorder) or when we break a law with which we don't agree. For example, we may not feel guilty when we break the law by jaywalking. We *are* guilty but don't *feel* guilty. On the other hand, we may *feel* guilty and yet not *be* guilty of a violation. We may feel terribly guilty if we were abused as a child. We *aren't* guilty, yet we *feel* guilty.

Our *sense* of guilt is based on feelings that may or may not be accurate, whereas our *state* of guilt is founded on the fact of our having committed a wrong.

Guilt is what we should experience when we do something wrong. It is a behavior-correcting device. *Guilt feelings* are what we experience when we think we've done something wrong. That is, we may experience guilt feelings both when we have and when we haven't done anything wrong. Malcom Jeeves said,

> When a psychotherapist speaks about guilt he almost always uses the word as short for "guilt-feeling," by which he means a psychological state or event. The theologian, on the other hand, in speak-

ing of guilt refers not to a feeling but to an objective ethical or forensic relation between a man and God, or between one man and another. To feel guilty and to be guilty are not the same thing: the two do not even necessarily exist in direct proportion. When the two meanings are confused, needless conflict is generated.[2]

Actual guilt is the result of a wrongdoing, a mistake or a blunder we committed. It may be our response to an obligation we neglected to fulfill. Whether a wrong has been committed or a good act omitted, we didn't behave as expected or commanded. This actual guilt is based on reality, on fact. We violated a known and accepted law. We transgressed. We blew it.

Our guilt feelings, on the other hand, may or may not be based on actual sin. They may be formed improperly, inappropriately and incorrectly. While we should experience feelings of guilt when we do commit an offense, many of us experience these haunting feelings when we have not actually engaged in wrongdoing.

There are several reasons we may experience excess guilt: we perceive we have erred when we haven't, our list of "wrong" or "sinful" behaviors is too extensive or legalistic, or we haven't totally appropriated God's forgiveness when we have sinned. When guilt feelings are recurring, chronic or continual, we are probably heaping needless guilt on ourselves.

If we determine our guilt by whether or not we *feel* guilty, we use a faulty decision-making system, because our feelings are unreliable indicators of whether or not we are actually guilty. *We can't rely on guilt feelings!*

In *Freedom from Guilt,* the authors state, "It's significant to note that of the three New Testament Greek words translated 'guilt' in our language *(hupodikos, opheilo,* and *enochos),* not one of them refers to the *feeling* of guilt. Instead, they mean 'to be liable to judgment,' 'to be guilty of an offense,' or 'to owe or be indebted to.' "[3] When God speaks of guilt he is referring to true, actual guilt, not an emotional state.

Where Guilt Comes From
One person in counseling sighed, "I can't remember a time when I haven't felt guilty for something!" Perhaps some of us identify with

that statement and would answer the question "When do you feel guilty?" with "All the time!"

Basically, we experience guilt feelings when we have done, or think we have done, something wrong.

We may feel guilty when

☐ we violate the law (legal guilt)

☐ we violate God's law (spiritual guilt)

☐ we violate our own principles, beliefs and expectations

☐ we fall short of meeting another person's expectations

☐ we violate a family tradition, value or expectation

☐ we violate a religious tradition, standard or expectation

☐ we violate a societal norm or cultural taboo

Some of these "violations" may trigger genuine guilt, while some may be accompanied by needless guilt.

The Role of the Conscience

Pinocchio's friend Jiminy Cricket takes the role of the conscience. He's the little voice that attempts to guide the adventurous wooden puppet along the right path in life. Like the conscientious cricket, the conscience is that part of us that serves as the sentinel for the beliefs, values, laws, aspirations and cultural taboos we seek to uphold. It represents our sense of right and wrong.

When we stray from what we regard as appropriate, acceptable, desirable, legal, moral or ethical, our conscience is supposed to set off an inner alarm, triggering guilt in hopes of preventing a transgression. Whenever an infraction is considered or committed, the conscience goes to work and sounds the sirens. Guilt is experienced whenever our thoughts, words or actions deviate from what we consider to be right.

The conscience, however, is not a foolproof warning device. It sometimes alerts us unnecessarily and sometimes neglects to trigger needed guilt when we have sinned. If our conscience is too tyrannical, we may punish ourselves without cause. If it is too lenient, we may commit grievous errors without a twinge of guilt. Dobson writes, "The conscience is an imperfect mental faculty. There are times when it condemns us for mistakes and human frailties that can't be avoided; at other times it will remain silent in the face of indescribable wickedness."[4]

We can think of the conscience as a computer programmed with volumes of rules, regulations and restrictions. This data comes from our families, faith and friends, as well as from our culture and our own expectations. *Our conscience responds to all of the data that has been inputted, not just to the truth of God's Word.* While some of the data is good (healthy and timeless), some needs to be examined and deleted because it is no longer applicable, is hazardous to our emotional or spiritual health or does not agree with the Word of God.

In order to deal with guilty feelings, we need to develop a good or clear conscience (1 Tim 1:5, 19; 3:9; 2 Tim 1:3; Heb 13:18), one that is sensitive to the Word of God and to the conviction of the Holy Spirit. Hebrews 9:14 declares, "How much more, then, will the blood of Christ, who through the eternal Spirit offered himself unblemished to God, cleanse our consciences from acts that lead to death, so that we may serve the living God!" Let's allow God to cleanse our consciences, deleting old, outdated, contradictory data and replacing it with the truth of his Word.

Without our conscience, as imperfect as it is, we would wander aimlessly, foolishly and dangerously, like a ship lost at sea. Our goal, then, is to have God's Word be the rudder to guide us and the breath of the Holy Spirit to fill our sails.

What Motivates Guilt

Our dutiful conscience is fueled by some of our deepest fears. These fears keep the conscience on twenty-four-hour watch over our thoughts and deeds. Without these fears we would become impervious to guilt's accusations. We feel guilty when we think our behavior has fallen short because we fear the possible outcome—the actualization of our fears.

Fear of punishment and pain. We fear that our wrongful thoughts and deeds may cause us to experience punishment and pain. We dread the possibility of personal humiliation and physical harm. As children we quickly learned that transgressing certain family rules resulted in

painful consequences. Our primitive sense of right and wrong developed based on what did and didn't receive strict disciplinary action.
Fear of rejection. We also fear that our misdeeds may cause rejection and alienation from others who will find us reproachable or undesirable. We strive toward a guiltless life in hopes that it will enhance our ability to be accepted by others. If we meet their standards and expectations, we decrease the possibility of feeling rejected and abandoned.
Fear of failure, worthlessness and incompetence. Last, we fear failure and feelings of worthlessness and incompetence. If we fulfill the rules and regulations set forth by society, our work, our faith and our family, we increase our feelings of competence and reduce our deep fear of being found to be a worthless human being.

The Difference Between Guilt and Shame
A friend of mine was baby-sitting a nephew. When the little boy disobeyed, my friend said, "Bad boy! Shame on you!" The preschooler got teary-eyed and said, "I'm not a bad boy; I just do bad things sometimes."

This little boy's parents taught him well—he is not a bad person if he does "bad things." Unfortunately, many of us do not make this same distinction. We often think that the two go hand in hand: if I do something wrong, then I am a bad person.

This confuses guilt and shame. Guilt declares that we have committed an error, while shame conveys the belief that we *are* an error. Guilt says, "I've done a bad thing," while shame says, "I am a bad person." Guilt focuses on the action, not the agent. To further illustrate the difference, "one might think of a boy who has committed a theft. The thief may feel guilty because he has violated a societal rule that he respects. And he may simultaneously feel ashamed because the act reduces his identity to that of a thief whom he imagines his parents, his friends and he himself would disrespect."⁵

With guilt, the "bad thing" we did is experienced as a reflection of a "bad decision." With shame, however, the "bad thing" is experienced as a reflection of a "bad self." *When guilt is excessive, chronic and viewed as a negative reflection of oneself, it becomes shame.*

Bad guilt can be much like shame in that we go beyond the sin to the sinner. Rather than hate the sin and love the sinner, as we are instructed to do, we hate the sin *and* hate the sinner—ourselves.

Good guilt tells us that we have committed an error and need to make amends. Good guilt focuses on our fallen nature's propensity toward sin and the need for a loving, forgiving God. It exposes our guilty nature but doesn't shame us. Bad guilt may cause us to feel guilty when we shouldn't and worthless when we aren't. "Most major psychological problems and symptoms are the result of an overload of destructive shame compounded by excessive false guilt."[6]

Good Guilt	*Shame*	*Bad Guilt*
Feelings regarding our sins	Feelings regarding our self	Feelings regarding our sins *and/or* self
Focuses on wrong committed	Focuses on wrong character	Focuses on wrong committed *and/or* character
Hate the sin	Hate the sinner	Hate the sin and the sinner
I did something bad	I am bad	I did something bad, therefore I might be bad
I made a mistake	I am a mistake	I think I made a mistake *and* might be a mistake
I'm worthy	I'm worthless	I'm not sure but I think I'm not worthy

When bad guilt is chronic or excessive, it appears similar to shame.

A theologian and counselor questioned, "Can you address guilt without addressing shame?" Though overlap exists between false guilt and shame, this book focuses on the complexities of guilt. In attacking guilt head-on I believe we are simultaneously attacking the parts of it that closely resemble shame. When we sin, God desires that we accept the fact of our guilt, confess, repent and receive his forgiveness. God's design not only frees us from guilt, it frees us from shame as well.

Application Questions
1. How would you define (or explain) guilt?
2. Which of the fears that motivate guilt do you struggle with?
3. What do you think is the difference between guilt and shame?
4. When do you experience guilt?
5. When do you experience shame?

Prayer
Lord, we praise you that you take away our guilt and shame. Please help us to feel guilty only when we are truly guilty and not to be haunted by unnecessary guilt feelings. Help us to be motivated by love for you, not fear. Help us to have a conscience guided primarily by your will and Word and not by our ways. Thank you. Amen.

F O U R

The Happy Ending

I enjoy watching movies. I like the entertainment, distraction, romance, action, mystery—and I like to study human behavior. Ever since becoming a psychologist, however, I rarely watch sad movies—those we call "tear-jerkers." Why? Because I deal with enough of life's difficulties and sadness in my counseling. I'm overloaded in the drama category and need more comedy, romance and action-adventure. I will occasionally watch an emotionally laden drama when I know ahead of time that it has a happy ending. Knowing the outcome helps me endure the sad parts of the movie.

This book is like that. Exposing our guilt may be painful and hard; acknowledging our sins can be a vulnerable and humbling ordeal. To uncover our counterproductive ways of dealing with guilt feelings can also be difficult, since we must admit that we have focused on our inadequacies rather than on God's adequacy. But even though it may be emotionally laden, I want you to know the ending ahead of time—it's happy.

Our happy ending is a result of the goodness of God, and it is this:

by his grace we can be free from guilt. As we unearth areas of hidden, unresolved or unnecessary guilt, we can hand it over to our Lord Jesus Christ, whose death on the cross takes away our sin and guilt. We don't deserve his forgiveness. We don't deserve to be washed white as snow (Is 1:18). We don't deserve his unfailing love. But we receive them—because of his grace.

Grace

Grace is receiving something we don't deserve. It is a gift that is unmerited and freely given. There is absolutely nothing we can do to earn this grace. No amount of good deeds can help us achieve God's favor. Ephesians 2:8 reminds us, "For it is by grace you have been saved, through faith—and this not from yourselves, it is the gift of God." Titus 2:11 adds, "For the grace of God that brings salvation has appeared to all." From these verses we learn that grace brings salvation, that it is not from ourselves or from anything we did or are, that it is a gift from God and that it is available to everyone. God's gift of grace to us occurs because of the death and resurrection of his Son Jesus Christ. His grace is freely given as our guilt-remover. "By hating sin, God shows justice. By forgiving sin, he shows mercy. But by *being the payment* for that sin himself, he shows matchless, marvelous, magnificent grace."[1]

In *Guilt and Grace*, the insightful and wise Swiss psychiatrist Paul Tournier writes, "God's free grace, which effaces guilt, runs up against the intuition which every man has, that a price must be paid. . . . God himself has paid the price once for all, and the most costly that could be paid—his own death, in Jesus Christ, on the Cross. The obliteration of our guilt is free for us because God has paid the price."[2]

Jesus showed us what he meant by grace when he welcomed sinners at his table, when he touched the banished leper, when he forgave the adulteress, when he allowed the children to come, when he told the story of the forgiven, restored prodigal son, when he spoke of the persistent woman, when he healed the sick, when he fed the multitudes and much more. He is a God who spared sin-ridden Nineveh, who loved an adulterous and idolatrous people and who used murderers and liars for his glory. His grace accepts the weak and the strong, the sinner and the saint, the prodigal and the faithful.

Warning

Have you ever had a minor surgery? Even though the procedure may have been considered quite safe, the doctor was required to inform you of any possible risks or complications. As we're going to examine the guilt in our lives and perform some internal surgery we should also be warned of things that might hinder our recovery and keep us from fully accepting God's free gift of grace.

In his wonderfully challenging and inspiring book *Grace Awakening,* Chuck Swindoll warns us against "grace killers." "There will always be those who will give us more and more and more to live up to. These are the grace killers whether they know it or not. By using guilt trips, shame techniques, and sneaky manipulations, they virtually drive us to distraction!"[3]

Our culture can kill grace. Well-meaning but rule-regulated Christians can be grace killers. Other grace killers include our fears, our attempts to earn God's favor, our insecurities and our renunciation of all pleasure. And hidden within all of these is guilt. Guilt tears us down and keeps us down. It pours water over our barely flickering embers, smothering our hope. It attacks us from all sides when we feel defenseless.

Guilt can't exist where grace abounds. Our goal is to be free in God's grace, not bound by our guilt.

Swindoll adds that we have a hard time experiencing God's grace "when our guilt and shame have not been adequately dealt with. Most folks, it seems, are better acquainted with their guilt and shame than with their God. Grace nullifies guilt. It renders shame powerless."[4]

Our unresolved guilt and guilt feelings may build a wall between us and God's grace. Perhaps we should post a sign: "Warning: the Great Physician has determined that guilt is hazardous to your spiritual health." By his grace, he has provided a way to remove that guilt.

Benefits

Before we proceed with a surgery, we consider not just the risks but also the benefits. Despite the warnings, we generally pursue the medical treatment because we consider it to be needed or beneficial to our health—that is, the benefits outweigh the cautions. So it is with our examination of guilt. Though the procedure might be painful, the end result is well worth it.

Becoming grace-filled rather than guilt-filled allows us to experience the true freedom that comes from knowing our Lord and Savior. John 8:36 proclaims, "So if the Son sets you free, you will be free indeed." We become free to concern ourselves with others' needs rather than our own. We are free from counterfeit Christianity with its rules, regulations and restrictions. We are free from the burden of others' expectations, opinions and obligations. We are free to experience the peace that comes from knowing his intimate and infinite love. Galatians 5:1 warns us not to lose our freedom: "It is for freedom that Christ has set us free. Stand firm, then, and do not let yourselves be burdened again by a yoke of slavery."

As we allow grace rather than guilt to rule our lives, we become more tolerant of others and ourselves. We become less selfish and more generous. Our time and energy are not spent hiding our guilt because we have already openly given it to our forgiving God. The hidden faults and sins that constantly harassed us lose their voice as we more clearly hear his soothing call.

The areas in our life that need cleansing are gently exposed in God's perfect timing. A friend told me, "I like to think of Jesus as the Master Electrician. When I turn my life over to him, he installs a light that helps expose the various parts of me that need cleaning. He doesn't turn the light on too bright at first, or I'd get overwhelmed with all of the dirt." I replied, "It sounds like he has a dimmer switch and gradually increases the light as we are able to handle the exposure of our sinfulness."

We need to expose our needless guilt in the light of his presence. We need to see it for what it is so that his grace can sweep it away.

Here's what we gain by embracing God's grace:

☐ We receive one blessing after another (Jn 1:16).

☐ We are saved (Acts 15:11; Eph 2:5, 8).

☐ We can be built up (Acts 20:32).

☐ We are justified (Rom 3:24; Tit 3:7).

☐ We have gained access to God by faith (Rom 5:2; Eph 2:8).

☐ We have eternal life (Rom 5:21).

☐ We are not under the law (Rom 6:14).

☐ Grace is available so that "in all things at all times, having all that [we] need, [we] will abound in every good work" (2 Cor 9:8).

☐ We can make it through times of weakness because his grace "is sufficient" (2 Cor 12:9).

☐ We have eternal encouragement and good hope (2 Thess 2:16).

☐ We don't have to do anything to earn his grace (Eph 2:8-9; 2 Tim 1:9).

☐ We can approach the throne of grace with confidence and receive mercy and help in time of need (Heb 4:16).

When I recently tuned in to a new radio station, the announcer talked about a contest that had been going on over the past few months. The grand prize, a trip to Hawaii, was to be given away to the person whose name he was about to draw. The drum roll began, and the winner's name was announced: Melissa MacFarlane. (At that moment I'm sure there were a lot of people who wished that was their name.) The disc jockey went on to say that in order to receive the prize, the winner needed to call the station within the next sixty minutes. If she didn't call and claim the prize, she wouldn't be able to enjoy the warm, sunny beaches of Hawaii.

God is on the radio, announcing each of our names, telling us that he has a priceless prize waiting for us. We, like Melissa MacFarlane, need to claim his gift of grace and enjoy the warmth of his forgiveness and love.

Grace Keepers

In the Disney movie *The Lion King*, the shocked and sad little lion cub is told by his evil uncle Scar that he is responsible for his father's death. Scar smothers Simba with guilt, adding, "What will your mother think?" When the future king asks, "What should I do?" sinister Scar replies, "Run away and never come back!"

Our pastor, Chip Ingram, recently used this illustration and then asked three questions: "First, is Simba guilty? That is, is he responsible for his father's death?"

"No," we all emphatically replied.

"Second, did he *feel* guilty?" We all nodded our heads in affirmation.

"And third, what can get rid of his guilt feelings?" Chip answered, "The truth," and he went on to tell us about God's amazing grace.

The truth on which we stand is found in the resurrected Christ. He conquered sin, taking our place on the cross so that our guilt and shame are removed. When the evil one tries to make us stumble in our guilt, we can stand firm on the Rock, unwavering in our knowledge that by his blood we have been freed from the guilt of our sins (Ps 32:5). How is our guilt taken away? By God's grace. We are to accept God's grace and grow in it, as Peter commands us: "Grow in the grace and knowledge of our Lord and Savior Jesus Christ" (2 Pet 3:18).

After reading the next few chapters, which help us identify obvious as well as inconspicuous guilt, we, like Simba, may want to run away and never come back. That may mean resorting to some coping mechanism, putting up a good front, running to addictive behaviors or falling into a "faith by works" (rather than grace) mentality.

If we focus on our guilt without simultaneously understanding God's grace, we may fall into despair. Both for the little lion cub and for us, the way to get rid of guilt feelings is to embrace the truth and let grace abound. We must become grace keepers.

Tournier suggests that as Christians more fully realize their imperfect nature and become disillusioned and discouraged by their perpetual sin, they begin to fathom God's grace. "It is then that we understand more profoundly how vast the grace is which receives us just as we are, with all our despair, all our weaknesses and all our relapses."[5]

If we don't embrace God's grace, we give in to guilt. When this happens, we become legalistic, tear others down and project guilt in order to help us feel better—we become grace killers and guilt producers. So as we continue to consider God's grace, let's examine not only the ways we need to shed excess guilt but also ways we may be directly or indirectly producing guilt in others. Let's strive to be people of grace rather than people of guilt. Let's be grace keepers and givers rather than grace killers and guilt producers.

The Highs and the Lows

As I recently read through the Psalms—something I love to do regularly—this wonderful verse in Psalm 36 stood out: "How priceless is your unfailing love! Both high and low among men find refuge in the shadow of your wings" (v. 7). Not only is God's unfailing love beyond measure and priceless, but it is available to the high and to the lowly.

Some people feel *low,* overwhelmed and burdened, unable to loose guilt's grip. They feel they are sinking in a sea of guilt. Others may feel relatively free, *high* above the crushing weight of guilt. Whether we find ourselves relatively unscathed by guilt or bathing in it, it is God's grace that has "brought us safe thus far, and grace will lead us home." When we are feeling victorious, successful, content or peaceful, it is because of his wondrous grace. When we are feeling downtrodden, discouraged and depressed, it is also by his grace that we are not defeated and destroyed.

The psalmist declares that whether we are rich or poor, royal or common, mature or immature, high or low, young or old, we can all find refuge in God. "The individual whose track record is morally pure has no better chance at earning God's favor than the individual who has made a wreck and waste of his life and is currently living in unrestrained disobedience. Everyone who hopes to be eternally justified must come to God the same way: on the basis of grace; it is a gift."[6]

No situation, no deed, no amount of guilt, no trouble, hardship or danger, nothing present nor in the future, no power—*nothing* can separate us from God's unfailing love (Rom 8:38-39). His grace reaches into the depths of our despair. His grace is more than sufficient to wipe away our guilt. His grace and his priceless unfailing love are given to *all* of us. The writer of Hebrews verifies this when he commands, "See to it that *no one* misses the grace of God" (Heb 12:15).

Read the words of this truth-telling hymn once again, with a fresh understanding and appreciation of his amazing grace.

> Amazing grace, how sweet the sound
> That saved a wretch like me!
> I once was lost but now am found,
> Was blind but now I see.

'Twas grace that taught my heart to fear
And grace my fears relieved.
How precious did that grace appear
The hour I first believed.

The Lord has promised good to me;
His word my hope secures.
He will my shield and portion be
As long as life endures.

Through many dangers, toils and snares
I have already come.
'Tis grace hath brought me safe thus far,
And grace will lead me home.

When we've been there ten thousand years,
Bright shining as the sun,
We've no less days to sing God's praise
Than when we'd first begun.

The Good News

Let's pretend we're on a football team that's about to face its toughest, meanest opponent. We study their plays and their players, their timing and their tricks. Fear sweeps through our team as we realize how overwhelming, ominous and foreboding this opponent is. We begin to feel scared and defeated. We want to give in and forfeit the game because we assume we're going to lose anyway.

But then the coach comes in and says that he knows the outcome of the game—we win! With renewed vigor, energy and excitement, we enter the field to play. The opponent is still fierce, the game is still rough, but we know that in the end we'll come out on top.

Our journey through guilt is like the preparation for that football game. We must study guilt's moves, traps and dangers—not to discourage or overwhelm us, but to help us "fight the good fight" (1 Tim 6:12). If we get overwhelmed by the amount of guilt we uncover in our motives, our behaviors and our emotions, we must not lose heart but lean on his sufficient grace (2 Cor 12:9). We still need to face the opponent, but we don't need to feel defeated or demoralized. Our coach, Jesus Christ, tells us the good news of assured victory. He encourages us not to give up or give in, even when life is tough and guilt overwhelms us. Because of what he's done on the cross, we've already won! Now that's a happy ending.

Application Questions
1. How would you explain grace to someone?
2. What other examples of God's grace, modeled by Jesus, can you add to those listed?
3. Which of the benefits gained from embracing guilt do you personally find most comforting?
4. What must we do to claim our prize, his gift of grace?
5. How do we become grace givers rather than grace killers? How do we avoid becoming guilt producers?

Prayer
Thank you, Lord Jesus, for your provision of grace. Help us not to be grace killers and guilt givers but people who are guilt killers and grace givers. We thank you that by your grace we have already won the battle against guilt. In your name, amen.

FIVE

Guilt Attacks

*W*e're so accustomed to guilt that we often don't see that it clouds our judgment, hinders our effectiveness and slows our progress. When we choose a certain product over another, guilt may motivate our decision. When we buy a more expensive gift than we'd originally planned, the extra expense may be due to guilt. When we subconsciously or consciously start avoiding a colleague, it may be guilt that is creating the distance.

I caught myself feeling guilty when a grocery clerk asked if I wanted my receipt. When I answered, "No," she replied, "But aren't you saving them for the school computer fund?" And what about the times I've been impatient with a slow driver in front of me, only to notice a disabled placard? Guilt also gets me when I look at my growing stack of unread magazines and unanswered letters.

A friend of mine said that she experienced how expensive guilt can be. She used to work in a dental office and knew how important it is to take good care of one's teeth. She felt so guilty for not flossing her teeth regularly that when she had a toothache, she decided not to go to the dentist right away. "I decided to put up with the pain until I could honestly tell my dentist that I'd been flossing faithfully for a month. When I finally went, he told me that I needed a crown and possibly a root canal. He went on to say it was too bad I hadn't come in sooner, because he could have saved the tooth. My guilt cost me a lot of money!"

One of my favorite comic-strip characters is Cathy. When she returns from an outing (probably shopping), she listens to the messages on her answering machine. One by one she is reminded of something she forgot to do or someone she forgot to call. The strip ends with Cathy stating, "For some, an answering machine. For me, a guilt machine."

One man's guilt at not being all his parents wanted him to be led him to be a driven workaholic. When his efforts resulted in numerous achievements and success, he then felt guilty because he felt he didn't deserve it. His situation illustrates a vicious cycle of guilt. Guilt led to drivenness, which resulted in success, which led to more guilt. For others, a related vicious cycle occurs when our guilt feelings lead to feelings of insecurity or anger, which causes us to feel more guilt, which then increases our insecurities and anger.

Guilt can be subtle and it can be simple. It can come and go and it can come and stay. Guilt can be triggered by little things, ordinary events and pleasant people, as well as by big things, extraordinary events and unpleasant people.

A man feels guilty about his wife's affair, a mother feels guilty about her teenage daughter's suicide, a businessman feels guilty about the company's failure and bankruptcy, and numerous Christians struggle with the guilt of doubting God. Many experience guilt because of their sexual longings. Grown children express guilt about feeling angry at their parents. One woman whose father died of cancer said, "I feel guilty for not dragging my father to the doctor sooner." Men and women express guilt about marital choices made impulsively or "on the rebound." Women struggle with having had abortions or giving up babies for adoption. Men face guilt when "success" is not achieved. One person summed up, "I want to stop feeling so guilty all the time. I just want to get on with life."

Guilt Target Zones

After Abraham Lincoln saw Niagara Falls for the first time, he was asked, "What made the deepest impression upon you?" With characteristic deliberation, Lincoln responded, "The thing that struck me most was, where in the world did all that water come from?" We could ask the same question regarding guilt: "Where is it all coming from?"

We are all different. We feel guilt differently, and we feel guilty about different things "because all of us have been differently conditioned by a host of factors—the ethnic and religious traditions of our parents and extended family, by the mores and standards of the society and culture around us, by playmates, teachers, peer groups."[1] Our life experiences and decisions have led us along different guilt paths. Even though our life journeys are unique and we feel guilt differently, we do share one commonality—we all experience guilt at one time or another, in one way or another.

The following is a list of some of the many ways we experience guilt, both in the daily grind and throughout our lifetime. Some of these will strike a familiar chord for you, while others may not. In which areas do you experience guilt? Do you ask yourself these questions? Do you tell yourself some of these things?

What we eat. Am I eating healthily? What about the calories and the fat, cholesterol, salt content? Should I eat this food? What about high blood pressure, excess weight and my cholesterol count? Is this on my diet?

Our relationships. I don't spend enough time with my friends, my spouse, my children, my parents. Miscommunications are all too common and communication is all too rare. I don't show enough appreciation and affection. I'm not as good a parent, friend, partner as I should be. My children don't respect me, and my parents say I'm ungrateful.

Our accomplishments. I never seem to complete my daily to-do list. Things just don't seem to get done as planned. I wish I could be more productive. I feel guilty when I don't do what I set out to do. Am I doing things just to gain acceptance?

Our religion. I should pray more, read my Bible more and go to church more regularly. I need to be more godly and more giving, more selfless and more serving.

Our aspirations. I should attain more, succeed more, be more. As one client said, "I'm surviving but not achieving."

Our use of leisure time. I often feel guilty about how I use my free time. Am I being a good steward of it? Am I being frivolous? Shouldn't I volunteer more rather than spend my time in selfish pursuits? When I relax I feel guilty—I feel I should be doing something more constructive.

Our health. I should exercise more, take better care of myself and eat healthy food. I should be better at following the doctor's recommendations.

Our parenting. I need to control my anger and be more patient with my children. When I'm not consistent I feel guilty because I know that's not good for them. I should spend more quality time with them.

Our regrets. My past is laden with events that I wish I could erase. I'm afraid of making similar mistakes and feel bad about those who were negatively affected before.

Our hobbies. I don't have enough hobbies or outside interests. Or I spend too much time and money on my hobbies. I should rearrange my priorities but I'm having a hard time giving up what I enjoy.

Our environment. I should be more aware of the environment and what I can do to help. I should be more diligent in recycling and in conserving energy.

Technology and our world. I should be more informed and up-to-date about the latest technology and what's happening in the world. I feel so ignorant.

Our time. I should use my time more wisely rather than waste it on television or other things. I need to have better self-discipline and time management.

Our resolutions. Another New Year's has come and gone, and I have yet to follow through on my resolutions. Why can't I fulfill my goals? I feel guilty when my resolutions fall by the wayside.

Our habits. I wish I didn't bite my nails. I wish I didn't smoke. It makes me feel guilty that I have this bad habit *and* that I can't seem to overcome it.

Our emotions. I wish I could control my temper. I wish I wasn't so sensitive and easily hurt. I should be more aware of others' feelings. Why do I struggle so much with jealousy and comparisons? Or with rage, insecurity, guilt?

Our decisions. I've made some bad decisions in the past. I need to be careful, not impulsive, in making decisions—especially those that affect others as well as myself.

Our selfishness. Society tells me that I deserve the best, but the Bible says I am to be selfless. I feel guilty whenever I do something for myself.

Our past. I feel guilty about my past and certain things that happened to me. If only I'd been stronger or more assertive. Why did I let those things happen? Why didn't I stop it? Why can't I seem to get on with my life?

Our situations. I should have married better. I should have moved when I had the chance—now I feel stuck. I blew my chance at ever getting a better-paying job. Why can't I change my situation?

One person sighed, "I feel guilty for feeling guilty all the time!"

Guilt and Our Personalities

In addition to the extensive list of possible guilt areas, our personalities can also generate guilt in a variety of ways, depending on where we live, what we do and who we know. In *The Dangers of Growing Up in a Christian Home,* the author reflects on listening to a dynamic Christian speaker.

Guiltily, I wondered what was wrong with me. Somehow the Christian life had never been as automatic or thrilling for me. Mine was more of a struggle. . . . In retrospect, I realized that [some people are] naturally emotional, easily excited, quick to be optimistic, and very good at talking excitedly about anything, whether it be Christ or a used car. In other words, a definite part of [the speaker's] meaningful salvation experience was due to his particular personality style. But in his well-intentioned enthusiasm to share his experience, he implied that everyone ought to feel the same way he did.[2]

What happens when we feel we don't "fit in," when our personality seems to be mismatched to our culture, our job or our family? We may wonder what's wrong with us and wish we were different. We may experience low self-esteem, low job morale, frustration and guilt.

Thomas felt guilty for not being more outgoing. Susie felt guilty for not enjoying her job. Patrice felt guilty for not being more creative, Martin for not being more logical. Many Christians, like the writer above, feel guilty for not being more outgoing, expressive, energetic and evangelistic.

An extrovert might feel guilty for being "different" in a culture where the reserved, nonassertive person is culturally esteemed. A shy introvert might feel guilty living in a country or family that prefers those who are outspoken, talkative and assertive.

In certain professions, those who are task-oriented are elevated in stature while in other work settings they would be ostracized for being impersonal and uncaring. Some jobs need people who prefer routine tasks, while other positions require individuals who enjoy changing challenges. In some work environments creativity is viewed as an asset, in others a liability.

Even within families, different personalities are present. Depending on the parents' temperament, children, to varying degrees, may feel like they don't fit in. The enthusiastic and energetic child may feel a bit out of place in a family of reserved parents. The artistically gifted child may feel guilty for being awkward and uninterested in sports.

Harry, an outgoing, sociable middle-aged man who came in for counseling, felt guilty for not being satisfied in his work. He was involved in a family bookkeeping company that required long hours alone with books and numbers. He felt bad for not enjoying his work and felt that he'd be letting the family down if he quit. His self-esteem was low, his guilt was high.

As we discussed his situation, a plan was devised. He decided to talk with the family about developing a new job description for him, focusing more on customer relations and new accounts. He offered to be the spokesperson whenever clients had questions or concerns and to go to various companies in an effort to develop new clients. His family was hesitant at first, but the changes were eventually made. Harry discovered that as both his morale and the number of new clients increased, his guilt decreased.

When we are mismatched with our job, our culture or our family, guilt usually pays a visit, hoping to set up permanent residence. We must not allow guilt to interfere with our ability to accept ourselves. Some areas in our personalities may need improving, but other parts need accepting. In order to fend off guilt attacks, we need to understand the strengths and weaknesses of who we are.

Assessing Our Guilt

As we begin to ask ourselves about when, where and how we feel guilty, we will become better able to fend off the unwanted attacks. The authors of *Guilt: Letting Go* write, "The only way we can stop being manipulated by unscrupulous advertisers, exploitive charities, tantalizing advertisements on television or in the newspapers, beggars and devious projections of guilt by our dearest friends, is to understand the roots of our own guilt and not let others use it against us."[3]

The following exercises can help you identify specific areas in which you feel guilty. So take out a pencil and paper and complete the following sentences.

1. I feel guilty when I

2. I feel guilty if I

3. I feel guilty when my mother

4. I feel guilty when my father

5. I feel guilty when my spouse

6. I feel guilty when my children

7. I feel guilty when my friend(s)

8. I feel guilty if I forget

9. I feel guilty when I don't

10. I feel guilty because

11. I feel guilty because I should

12. I feel guilty if/when I eat

13. I feel guilty about exercising because

14. I feel guilty about the way I use my time when

15. I feel guilty with God when

16. I feel guilty when I disappoint

17. I feel guilty if I can't

18. I feel guilty when I make decisions/choices that

19. I feel guilty when I miss the opportunity to

20. I feel guilty if I go ahead and

21. I can't

22. I wish

This next list also helps us clarify how often we feel guilty in a variety of areas. Check those areas in which you experience guilt and to what degree.

M = much of the time   S = some of the time   R = rarely

1. I feel guilty about my relationship with God. _____
2. I feel guilty about my work performance. _____
3. I feel guilty about my relationship with my parents. _____
4. I feel guilty about my relationship with my spouse. _____
5. I feel guilty about my parenting skills. _____
6. I feel guilty about feeling guilty. _____
7. I feel guilty about what I'm not doing about the environment. _____
8. I feel guilty about how I spend my time. _____
9. I feel guilty about how/what I eat. _____
10. I feel guilty about my lack of achievements. _____
11. I feel guilty about some unwanted habits. _____
12. I feel guilty when I feel angry or jealous. _____
13. I feel guilty when I have fun. _____
14. I feel guilty about giving in to temptation. _____
15. I feel guilty about unconfessed sin. _____
16. I feel guilty about my Christian walk. _____
17. I feel guilty when I neglect prayer. _____
18. I feel guilty when I spend money. _____
19. I feel guilty when I do things for myself. _____

20. I feel guilty about my weight. _____
21. I feel guilty about _____ . _____

    Answers to this checklist and the sentence completion exercise help us answer our question about guilt, "Where in the world does it all come from?" The following chapters further expose some of the major areas of our lives in which guilt gets a foothold. We will examine how we developed guilt growing up in our families, the many ways that guilt and religion go together, and how expectations and our culture contribute to our guilt feelings.

Application Questions
    1. In the first list, check those areas in which you experience guilt. Are there other areas in which you experience guilt? Were you surprised at how few or how many areas you identified with?
    2. In what ways does your personality allow guilt to infiltrate your emotions? What aspects of your personality are most prone to guilt attacks?
    3. If you haven't already done so, complete the sentences in the first survey. Did you learn or realize anything new about yourself and ways you experience guilt? Are you surprised at any of your answers? Do you notice any similar responses or patterns (for example, that most of your guilt has to do with family, your relationship with God or your expectations)?
    4. If you haven't already done so, complete the second survey on frequency of guilt. In which areas did you mark "some of the time"? "much of the time"?

Prayer
Lord, please help us identify those areas in which we feel guilty so that we may get rid of the excess, bad guilt and pay attention to the good guilt which forces us to our knees before you. Amen.

SIX

Family & Guilt

Randy sought counseling because of depression and low self-esteem. When I asked him to tell me about his childhood memories, they were filled with horror stories of physical and emotional abuse. Both parents continually gave him messages such as "You're so dumb, you'll never amount to anything" and "You're a bad boy! Can't you do anything right?" Once his mother shattered a coffee mug on his head. As Randy began to disclose his past, his guilt level seemed to increase. Even though he was beginning to understand the abusive nature of his parents' acts, he continued to struggle with guilt feelings. "I feel guilty for being angry at my parents," he said. "There's something inside me that says I should be grateful for what they did *for* me, that I shouldn't be mad at them for what they did *to* me."

Shara was also abused as a child—sexually abused by her father. She reported feeling guilty most of her childhood, assuming that the abuse was her fault. As she worked through the abuse and began to gain personal strength, she developed some strict guidelines for when and how long she would visit her parents with her own young children.

Family members ostracized her for not forgiving and forgetting the past. Even though she knew in her mind that the boundaries she'd established were right and healthy, she was often overcome with guilt feelings. "I feel guilty for having these rules, when it's not even my fault that I had to set them up in the first place!"

With regard to home-grown guilt, survey respondents said that they feel guilty "when I disappoint my parents and don't live up to their standards," "when my parents give advice and I don't heed it," "when my parents hint about wanting me to come visit and I don't enjoy spending time with them," "when my mother and father don't agree with a decision I've made," "when my mother's insulting jabber gets on my nerves" and "when my parents speak harshly to me."

Glenda sought counseling for anxiety. As we talked about the root of her fears, she continually referred to her parents' pessimistic attitude. In one of our first few sessions she stopped midstream and said, "I feel so guilty for talking negatively about my parents."

Homegrown Guilt

Who can make you feel guilt faster than anyone in the world? Probably your mother . . . followed closely by your father, Aunt Minnie, your sisters and brothers, grandparents and any other assorted relatives you may have scattered around. Parents definitely have the edge, though, when it comes to making the average adult child feel guilty. . . . It's lucky parentally-induced guilts don't pop out like boils. Most of us would be unable to sit down.

How do they [our parents] do it? How can they make us feel guilty so easily? It's simple: they are parents, and no matter how old we are, we are always their children. They are accustomed to telling us what to do, and we're accustomed to responding.[1]

How we were raised is a major factor in the development of our sense of guilt. Our parents or guardians instilled within us certain rights and wrongs we needed to function within both the family unit and society. Even though we are all born with the capacity to feel guilt, our parents taught us what to feel guilty about. We were taught what to do, how to do it and when it was and wasn't appropriate to do it.

In order to gain our compliance, our parents generally encouraged us with approval and rewards or coerced us with punishment, fear or threats. To disobey meant to face possible pain, humiliation or loss. When we disobeyed a well-established family rule, we suffered the consequences, which may have been the loss of a privilege, a "time out," a look of disapproval or a spanking.

If our parents were successful enough, they were able to instill in us not just the fear of punishment but also a sense of guilt or remorse if we failed to obey. In a sense, our conscience was being programmed to trigger guilt whenever our parents weren't around. It served as either a time clock or a time bomb. "A person's conscience is largely a gift from his parents—from their training and instruction and approval and disapproval. The way that right and wrong are taught throughout the first decade of life will never be completely forgotten—even though it may be contradicted later."[2]

Morgan said, "I don't understand why I still value my parents' opinions so much. I hear them all the time, in everything I do. They're like a shadow that is behind me all the time."

The Parents' Job

The other day my young daughter asked me, "What do parents do? What's their job?" I thought about it, then answered, "Our job is to love you no matter what, to help you know God, to tell you what is dangerous and to teach you what is right and what is wrong."

If our parents loved us conditionally, we felt guilty when they withheld their love. If we strayed from doing what was right, we felt guilty for our misbehavior. It is primarily this latter parenting "job" that contributes most to the development of our sense of guilt. Our parents were the conveyors of right and wrong—givers of praise and bestowers of punishment. A large part of our capacity to embrace guilt was inculcated in us by our parents. After our parents told us that something was wrong, we felt guilty when we did it—and sometimes even when we thought about it.

As I reflected on my daughter's question and my answer, I was struck by the awesome task parents face. In order to "teach you what is right and wrong," parents also have to decide

☐ What *is* right and what *is* wrong?

☐ What is important and what is not? (What is situational or family-specific, and what is moral, eternal and socially invaluable?)

☐ How should parents instill or teach these rights and wrongs?

There are many ways parents can err. They could do well in most of these areas and still produce guilt-ridden children and adults.

It is every parent's duty to impart to children social etiquette and morals. We were taught not to lie, but also not to chew food with our mouth open. We were instructed in the importance of sharing our toys, but also in the need to take off our muddy shoes outside. We were told not to steal, not to swear *and* not to leave our dirty clothes on the floor.

Some of these "appropriate" behaviors reflect underlying moral and religious principles—honesty, sharing, kindness—while others are societal rules of etiquette and situational or family-specific preferences. To further complicate matters, some behaviors are considered acceptable at one age and wrong at another. At two years of age our children were not allowed to answer the phone or to chew gum, but when they became older they could do both.

Right and wrong can change with age, family and situation. After we put new carpet in our family room, I made a rule that shoes were to be removed before anyone entered that part of the house. While visiting a friend's home our young son proclaimed, "Mom, they're doing a 'no-no.' They didn't take their shoes off." I then tried to explain that different families have different "no-nos"—which wasn't an easy task with a three-year-old!

Not only is our sense of right and wrong determined by family-specific rules, but it may also be culture-specific. In some cultures, for example, it is considered rude if one doesn't belch loudly after a meal. This behavior, considered extremely offensive in our culture, is a high compliment to the cook, indicating satisfaction with the food.

Children see life concretely, in terms of black and white, right and wrong. They don't see the difference between important social values, morals, religious beliefs and family-specific preferences, between lying and taking off muddy shoes. To them, both are wrong, and both lead to some sort of negative repercussion.

As grown children we generally forget to filter all of these rights and wrongs through an adult mentality. We perpetuate what we were taught without questioning whether it is applicable now. We often retain values, rules and beliefs that should have been shed long ago.

If we were raised in a home where wearing high heels, going to the movies and playing cards were wrong, should we continue to consider these actions "wrong," or should we decide for ourselves? Some of the rights and wrongs we learned are timeless, such as not to lie, steal or murder, but others are variable and must be examined. We experience excess guilt when we hang on to outdated concepts of what is acceptable and what is not.

How Children Think

Children tend to blame themselves whenever there are problems or family failures. They generally view parents as all-knowing and incapable of making mistakes. If problems do exist, they assume that they must somehow be responsible—guilty. Whether or not guilt is induced by parents, it is already a part of a child's makeup to assume it. This is evidenced by the children who say, "I feel guilty when my dad is mad," "I felt guilty when our cat died," "I felt guilty when my parents got a divorce." They think, *Maybe if I cleaned my room better or got better grades Dad wouldn't be mad,* or *If I hadn't lied about my lunch money, Mom and Dad wouldn't be getting divorced.*

Piaget's theory of cognitive development states that children think egocentrically *(everything, including problems, revolves around me).* A counseling colleague remarked, "Adults sometimes carry this form of thinking into adulthood, which keeps them developmentally stuck. They still think that most problems are their fault."[3] The authors of *Guilt: Letting Go* write,

> We've met people who have truly manipulative, rotten parents. They know it and . . . yet . . . they keep going back for more. . . . When we ask why, they explain that they feel it must be their own fault. Somehow, they should be able to find a way to make it work one of these days, if only they keep trying. It must be some personal sin that causes their parent to be so hateful.[4]

How Children Learn Right from Wrong

Lawrence Kohlberg proposed a theory of development that seeks to explain how and why we learn moral behavior. He found that very young children learn and obey rights and wrongs in order to avoid punishment. That is, we obeyed our parents not because it was the right thing to do but in order to avoid the negative consequences.

As we grew older, preschool to early elementary school age, our motive for doing what was right was based on the rewards or benefits we derived from such behavior. That is, the actions that were "morally right" to us at this stage were those that met our own needs, brought us pleasure and perhaps brought us candy or money as well.

Older still in the elementary years, we obeyed the rules—again, not because we necessarily considered them to be morally right, but in order to please others and be viewed as a good girl or a good boy. Our goal at this stage was familial and societal conformity and acceptance. We learned that pleasing others brought rewards, positive feedback and a sense of fitting in.

At the next stage of moral development, Kohlberg states, we obey rules and regulations because it is expected, mandatory and necessary in keeping the social order. Restrictions are viewed somewhat as absolutes, not to be questioned. This thinking fuels much of the legalism that I will discuss later.

While Kohlberg's theory continues to explain why we adhere to moral values in later life, a look at our formative years will suffice. In summarizing this theory of moral development for the younger years, we see that our motivations were as follows:

1. We obeyed due to fear of punishment.

2. We obeyed for the rewards we got for obeying (greed, materialism, pleasure).

3. We obeyed in order to please others (to avoid rejection and loneliness and to gain love, approval and acceptance).

4. We obeyed because it was necessary to maintain order and control.

As our parents sought to teach us the distinction between what is right and what is wrong, they employed these tactics—fear of punishment, rewards, love and acceptance, and legalism. Some used these strategies effectively, and some used them in ways that contributed to the development of false guilt. Unfortunately, none of us grew up with flawless parents who disciplined us perfectly. Whether loving or demeaning, our parents sometimes punished us in anger, motivated us by guilt and rejected *us* along with our undesirable behavior.

Parenting Problem 1: Deciding What Is Right and What Is Wrong
Let's examine the decisions facing parents in their efforts to teach
morals to their children. First they must decide what *is* right and what
is wrong. How is this decided? Unnecessary guilt may ferment in the
family that is too legalistic in their definitions and decisions of what
they consider to be right and wrong. Whereas parents need to foster
some sense of guilt in order to bring about positive behavior change,
imposing excessive guilt on children may well produce guilt-ridden
adults.

Suppose you were raised by parents with too rigid a perspective of
what is wrong. You grew up with a sense that most things were wrong
and few things were okay. Life was like a minefield, and you grew up
afraid to walk for fear that you would trip an explosion. This overly
inclusive conception of guilt-producing behaviors contributes not only
to guilt-prone adults but also to a lack of excitement for life. Life
seems to have more taboos than treats, more pitfalls than pleasures.
If the scope of incorrect, unacceptable behavior was too broad while
you were growing up, guilt generally flooded in.

Parenting Problem 2: Deciding What Is Important and What Is Not
Parents' failure to clearly delineate between consequential and incon-
sequential wrongs—which behaviors are deplorable and which are
simply not desirable—leaves another open door to guilt. If you grew
up in such a home, neglecting to feed the pet, stealing a candy bar from
the store, missing five items on a spelling test and lying to a teacher
all might have been treated as major calamities and punished with
equal severity. Distinctions weren't clear as to what was and was not
important. You grew up in fear of making any mistake and feverishly
sought never to err.

If as a child we develop a sense that every offense is a major one,
we carry that into adulthood. All failures are seen as catastrophes. All
errors in judgment are monumental. All relationship problems are of
seismic proportions. There are no little wrongs, only big ones. The
effect of this indiscriminate thinking is devastating. We become immobilized, fearing failure at every turn. This paralysis is accompanied by
guilt—the ghosts of guilt past, present and future.

I have found it helpful to ask myself, *How would Jesus view this behavior? Would he condemn me as much as I am condemning myself?* Recall the woman caught in adultery. The culture of that day considered her adulterous behavior to be a major sin, deserving of death. Jesus, however, didn't stress the size of the offense or condemn her for her sin. He simply told her to go and discontinue the undesirable behavior.

Parenting Problem 3: Deciding How to Teach Rights and Wrongs
Throughout history people have used a variety of methods for teaching and imparting beliefs. Ideas have been modeled, taught, encouraged, indoctrinated, coerced and forced. While some of these methods are productive, they may also be harmful. A parent's job is to determine which techniques are both effective in producing the desirable outcome *and* nontoxic.[5] Let's examine some of the common ineffective tools our parents used to convey their ideas of right and wrong—and ingrain our sense of guilt.

Emotional control/manipulation. Perhaps you were raised in a family where control was imposed through guilt manipulation. "If you don't do this, then it must mean you don't love your mommy and daddy." Or, "Because you didn't do this, I'm getting a headache" (it's all *your* fault). Or, "You have to do this if you want to be a good person."

Such statements convey the idea that if we don't respond to others and do things for them, we don't care about them, or if we don't do something they request, we will be the cause of their grief and difficulties. The idea is communicated that we alone are responsible for their pain. If they are displeased or in pain, we are the guilty culprit. Another idea communicated in these manipulative statements is that the only way to be a useful, good, productive person is to do whatever we are told or asked to do. We learn that we are loved and accepted as long as we meet certain conditions.

Spiritual manipulation. In an effort to obtain children's obedience, some parents use God. Teaching children that they "had better behave because Jesus is watching your every move" creates fear and a belief that God is a strict, easily displeased ogre. In *The Dangers of Growing Up in a Christian Home,* Donald Sloat writes, "One of the most harmful practices in evangelical homes is parents' use of God and

Scripture to control children, avoid personal responsibility, and justify negative child-rearing practices."[6]

Anger. The use of anger to instill beliefs about what is right and wrong is as ineffective as it is harmful. Obedience may be obtained, but not without negative repercussions such as overt rebellion, hate, passivity, fear, guilt or rejection. The price is high, and yet many parents still use this method, whether by choice or by habit.

If you came from a home in which anger was a tool for obedience, you may feel guilty in several ways. First, whenever you now experience anger you may be overcome with guilt, since you swore you'd never be like that. Second, you may feel guilty (responsible) for causing your parent to lose his or her temper. (Remember, as children we tended to accept responsibility for our parents' behavior. This often carries over into adulthood.) And last, you may feel guilty for the anger you feel toward your parent(s). Anger is a very effective guilt-producing method.

The silent treatment. Another method parents use in their effort to ensure obedience is silence. Children from these homes come to dread silence, preferring a harsh spanking or a strong reprimand. In these families silence is a shaming device because it is interpreted as "You are bad" (shame) and not simply "You did bad" (guilt). The silent treatment, ironically, often speaks louder than words.

The negative side effects from homes where silence was used are numerous—a sense of shame (personal worthlessness), conditional love and acceptance, fear of rejection and abandonment, to name a few. In adulthood, when awkward silences occur in relationships, we assume that something is wrong *and* we are the ones who did the wrong. All silences are then interpreted as direct communication of disapproval and disappointment.

Fear of punishment. Kohlberg's theory of moral development proposes that children first learn values, rules, morals and parentally desirable beliefs because they fear the punishment that accompanies divergence from them. Punishment may take the form of physical discipline, verbal abuse, a time-out, loss of a privilege or a chore to fulfill. Charles H. Spurgeon said, "A child's back must be made to bend, but not be broken. He must be ruled, but not with a rod of iron. His spirit must be conquered, but not crushed." Unfortunately, many well-meaning parents crush their children's spirits with their harsh disciplinary methods.

If our parents' use of punishment was excessive, then our sense of guilt may also be excessive because we come to expect punishment for all of our transgressions—whether big or small, real or imagined, in deed or in thought. The resulting unhealthy adults generally fall into two types. First, there are those who avoid exposure of their wrong-doings at all costs—even at the cost of honesty and personal integrity. Why pay such a high price? Because they have become accustomed to covering up the misdeed in order to avoid the devastating penalty.

Second, since many of our transgressions are known only to us, our burden of guilt weighs even more heavily unless we find ways to punish ourselves. "When our parents are no longer present to punish our misdeeds, a problem arises: how can this anxiety be alleviated? Years of discipline have taught us, 'When you're wrong, you must be punished.' Even in our parents' absence this nagging thought persists. To relieve this anxiety, we develop intricate ways of inflicting punishment on ourselves."[7] Our self-imposed punishment may take many different forms including substance abuse, self-deprivation, self-mutilation, clumsiness, forgetfulness or lack of pleasurable pursuits.

Reward system. Referring again to Kohlberg's theory, we find that children are also motivated toward appropriate behavior when they believe they can benefit from such behavior. Though this can be an effective system, it produces guilt byproducts when parents use it excessively. As adults, when we are given gifts or other tokens of friendship and affection, guilt often questions us: *Did you earn that? What did you do to deserve that?* Rewards are either guilt-producing, because they feel undeserved and unearned, or suspect, as we ask ourselves, *What does the person want or expect? What am I supposed to do?* Our lives are held hostage by these questions rather than freed to appreciate others' tokens of appreciation.

Fear of disapproval. Kohlberg states that older children may behave in order to please adults and to gain approval. They desire to be considered a "good girl" or a "good boy." This desire can be harnessed to develop good behavior if used constructively. Unfortunately, many parents use this fear in ways that are destructive and guilt-inducing.

If we came from homes that associated our worth with our approval rating, we may have self-esteem that resembles a roller-coaster ride. One day we were approved and considered a "good kid." But if we disobeyed the next day, we fell from our parents' grace and received the scorn of disapproval. Daily and weekly ups and downs taught us that our worth was determined by our deeds. Perhaps we became perfectionists in an effort to win the battle of approval. Or perhaps we became rebellious because the fight seemed hopeless. Gaining our parents' approval seemed like an overwhelming, ever-changing challenge. We may have dug in for a long battle, surrendered early, retreated or defected.

Fear of rejection or abandonment. "Some parents find that withdrawal of love is a quick way to enforce good behavior. Faced with the consequence of losing love, most of us try to change to please the ones we love."[8] Fear of rejection is one of the most powerful of all human emotions. The fear of losing love, of being abandoned, rejected and left alone runs deep in our veins.

If this fear was used to gain compliance when we were children, we may suffer devastating consequences throughout adulthood. We may experience difficulties in relationships, being overly dependent, having poor boundaries and lacking or fearing intimacy. We may have difficulties with self-acceptance, anger, guilt, trust, anxiety or depression. We may become fearful of people, relationships or commitment. We may shut off our emotions, or we may open the floodgates haphazardly.

Right and wrong were instilled in us in ways that were either right or wrong. And reprogramming parent-initiated guilt usually takes some time.

The Guilt of Growing Up

"My mom never liked anything I liked," Danielle said. "All that dislike of the things I like caused a tremendous amount of guilt, which later led to my constantly trying to be a people pleaser. Or I went the opposite way and became a rebel. I'm still trying to figure out who I am and what I really like and believe in."

According to Erik Erikson's theory of psychosocial development, we go through various stages as we grow. At each stage we have a task to fulfill. If the task isn't attained, we carry this unfinished burden with us throughout life until it is resolved. The task during adolescence is to search for and find some sense of personal identity apart from our parents. Unfortunately, some parents find this distasteful, not wanting little Joey to grow up and be independent. Whether or not our parents put this sort of pressure on us, we may have experienced guilt—the guilt of growing up.

The growing-up process meant separating ourselves from our parents—making our own decisions, choosing our own values and grappling with critical life issues by ourselves. We wanted to become "grown-up." General Hershey once said, "A boy becomes an adult three years before his parents think he does, and about two years after he thinks he does."[9]

In order to accomplish this critical task of becoming our own person (a task known as individuation), we had to devalue our parents. We may have felt angry at our parents for their rules and restraints. We may have viewed them as "old-fashioned" or "stupid." Mark Twain wrote, "When I was a boy of fourteen, I thought my father was ignorant. But when I got to be twenty-one, I was astonished at how much he'd learned in seven years." These feelings and thoughts, and the myriad others experienced as a part of growing up and out, are generally accompanied by guilt.

Becoming our own person is hard. We may feel guilty about our growing autonomy and independence because we convict ourselves of being overly rebellious and ungrateful. We may incorrectly believe that in order to develop our own values and beliefs we must defy and dishonor our parents.

> Too often parents [of adolescents] not only maintain the decision-making power for themselves, but also make their children feel so guilty about questioning their judgment that the children are afraid to challenge their parents' viewpoints. . . . Parents may instill so much fear and guilt along with values that youngsters are afraid to sort out their beliefs in order to stand on their own. . . .
>
> [Another] problem exists when youngsters accept what their parents have taught them without questioning or evaluating it. They are then simply following hollow beliefs that can crumble easily under pressure. This is especially true when Christian parents either do not teach children to think for themselves or do not even allow

them to do so. . . . As a result they live out traditions that have little or no personal meaning.[10]

Differing from our parents doesn't mean that we destroy our relationship or that we are unspiritual or ungrateful. It simply means that we are becoming independent, struggling to discover who we are. The guilt of growing up can exist with "good" parents as well as "bad" parents. We experience guilt simply because we are developing into our own person apart from our parents.

Reexamining the "Right and Wrong" List

If we find ourselves feeling excessive guilt, we do well to examine our list of what is right and wrong in order to see if we have some unwanted and unnecessary baggage. Many items on the list will need to stay, but there may be quite a few that need tossing.

If we were raised in homes where excessive guilt was engendered in order to gain control, many areas in our lives may be affected.

☐ Were there too many restrictions, prohibitions, rules and regulations?

☐ Did we become afraid of doing anything for fear of retribution?

☐ Were all offenses major ones?

☐ Did we grow up afraid of making mistakes?

☐ Did our parents' response to our misbehavior leave us feeling ashamed, guilt-ridden, stupid, rejected, conditionally loved, worthless, angry and/or afraid of God?

If you answered yes to any of these questions, most likely you are carrying around some excess guilt that should be discarded. It has weighed you down too long and has slowed your pace in life. As you cast it off, you'll discover how much easier it can be to walk through life without this unwanted burden.

Our Responsibility

Parents generally serve as our sometimes deserving and sometimes undeserving scapegoats. Not long ago I read a research report that verified adults' tendency to blame their parents, especially their mothers, for their problems. Social scientists who have studied the nature-nurture controversy generally conclude that we are a product of both our nurturing (environment) and our nature (innate personality traits).

Although we may find fault with the way our parents raised us, we must not blame them for all of our inadequacies and weaknesses.

Some parents are wonderful; some are abusive. Whatever type of parents we had, we need to remember that they are not perfect. In fact, parents cannot give what they themselves never had. This realization provides room for a lot of grace and forgiveness and improves our ability to move on.

It is true that our parents have played a large role in the development of our sense of guilt. But rather than blame them for our shortcomings, we must strive to overcome the harm and negative side effects. Professional or pastoral counseling may be needed to help us sift through the rubble of our past, to clear away the debris. Our goal must be to take control of and responsibility for ourselves rather than live a guilt-ridden, bitter, blame-projecting life.

Parenting Guilt

Much of this chapter has focused on the guilt we *derived from* our parents. This section will take a look at the guilt we *develop* as parents.

Survey respondents gave the following answers for "I feel guilty . . .":

☐ when I don't spend enough time with my children

☐ when I'm impatient with my children and blow up at them

☐ when I lie to my children in order to make them obey

☐ when I discipline my child too harshly

☐ when I'm too lenient

☐ when I let my children watch too much television or videos

☐ when I don't keep my promises to my kids

☐ when I am inconsistent in disciplining my children

☐ when I can't go to all my kids' activities

☐ when my children make mistakes or don't behave properly

☐ when one of my children talks back to me

☐ when my grown children ask me to baby-sit and I say no

☐ when my grown children have problems

☐ for working and leaving my child in daycare all day

We parents can't win. There is always something we feel we could or should be doing. One parent feels guilty because she can't afford to give her children their favorite cold cereal. Another feels guilty for having cold cereal because "a good mom takes the time to fix hot cereal and to give her kids a warm start on the day." One woman wrote, "I felt guilty for not having the cookie jar full all the time. I had this idea that a 'good mom' does that. When I finally started making homemade cookies every week I also started feeling a new guilt—guilt for letting my children have too many sweets. I can't win; I feel guilty either way!"

The author of *What Kids Need Most in a Mom* writes,

Oh, and guilt—guilt is like an addiction to so many moms. . . . Commercialism has made Mother's Day the greatest contributing factor to guilt in this century. . . . How can a mother read the flowery descriptions of what we're supposed to be and not feel guilty? According to the cards, mothers are *sunshine, laughter, moonlight and roses.* Mothers are *ever faithful, enduring, strong and compassionate.* Quite frankly, verses on Mother's Day cards make me want to . . . throw up.[11]

Perfect parenting doesn't exist, just as perfect kids don't exist. And yet we still heap unnecessary guilt onto ourselves for every perceived infraction. In the above list of survey responses, only a few of the "guilts" represent what I would consider to be good guilt. We should not lie to our children, we should keep our promises, we should make our kids a priority, we should control our anger, and we should strive for fair and consistent discipline. Most of the other responses represent preferences, not absolutes. These are the guilts we need to avoid.

Excess guilt is wasted energy, emotional energy that could be spent on our kids. Our job as parents is to experience true guilt and to eliminate false guilt.

One father wrote, "As I raise my own kids I don't want to lay guilt trips on them, but since I've never completely come to terms with the way my parents did it, I continue to do it to my kids." It is impossible to raise children without implanting or fostering some degree of guilt. Our challenge is to minimize the amount of false guilt—guilt over needless and useless things, both in our children and in ourselves. We need to be free of counterproductive guilt, and we need to encourage that same freedom in our children.

Application Questions
1. What methods did your parents use to teach you what was right and wrong?
2. In what ways did your upbringing contribute to your guilt and affect your life?

a. Were there too many restrictions, prohibitions, rules and regulations?

b. Did you become afraid of doing anything for fear of retribution? Were all offenses major ones? Did you grow up afraid of making mistakes?

c. Did your parents' response to your misbehavior leave you feeling ashamed, guilt-ridden, stupid, rejected, conditionally loved, worthless, angry and/or afraid of God?

3. If you are a parent, here are some questions to help you review your job description:

a. How are you deciding what is right and wrong and what moral and religious values you want your children to learn? Which values and rules are important and which are family-specific, flexible or age-specific?

b. How do you discipline? Do you use discipline methods that are detrimental and destructive or caring and constructive?

c. How do you encourage personal growth and yet remain in the parental role? How much do you loosen the boundaries/rules as your children get older? Do you allow your children to question your values as they seek to develop their own sense of identity?

4. How will you avoid the many parenting pitfalls that contribute to unhealthy, guilt-ridden adults?

Prayer
Our Father, we need your help as we seek to sort out our past and any areas in which we may be allowing guilt a negative foothold. Help us also to minimize the excessive guilt we may directly or indirectly be passing on to our children. Thank you. Amen.

SEVEN

Religion & Guilt

*O*n August 1, 1980, I was struck by lightning while working at a Christian camp. After my shocking experience, I was asked by numerous people, "Why do you think God did that?" Others, half-joking and half-serious, asked, "What did you do wrong?"

I don't know why it happened (although I *was* in the wrong place at the wrong time), but I do know this—I asked myself the same questions. What particular sin had I committed to warrant this electrifying experience? I foolishly viewed God as the Great Punisher who is ready to strike us whenever we sin. My view of God was askew.

> Who can make you feel guilty faster than your parent? Only God
> . . . or the childhood images of Him most of us learned from
> parents, the clergy, the nuns, and our Sunday School teachers. We
> were taught God had immense power over our lives, and immense
> expectations. But as children, we couldn't seem to be that good,
> that holy, that perfect, and most of us were doomed to failure and
> guilt before we ever finished memorizing the rules.[1]

Unfortunately, many of us experience more guilt than God in our lives. Our religion is thus founded on fear rather than faith. We view

God as an unrelenting taskmaster with whip in hand. He becomes a God who is displeased with pleasure and disapproving of disobedience. He is seen as demanding, domineering and difficult. He becomes more a God of wrath than a God of wonder—a God of guilt rather than a God of grace. When we overemphasize our sin, our guilt causes us to run *from* God rather than *to* him.

Religion and Guilt

A Jewish rabbi wrote, "You don't have to be Jewish to be an expert in guilt. Catholics often outdo Jews in their ability to create guilt . . . [and] even long after Martin Luther and Jonathan Edwards, Protestants still know guilt. And Moslems, too. What do these religions have in common? Guilt. We are all experts on guilt."[2]

Regardless of our religious heritage, most of us experience feelings of guilt in one way or another.

> Think of the innumerable multitudes of Hindus who plunge into the waters of the Ganges to be washed from their guilt. Think of the votive offerings and the gold-leaf which covers statues of the Buddha. Think of all the penitents and pilgrims of all religions who impose upon themselves sacrifices, ascetic practices, or arduous journeys. They experience the need to pay, to expiate.[3]

Different times produce different guilt, and churches espouse a variety of guilt-producing ideas. Whether it is in tithing, serving, studying or obeying, we have many opportunities to experience religiously related guilt.

A friend said that when she attended a well-respected Christian college, the emphasis was on getting a job in the secular workforce in order to be a witness to non-Christians. When another friend attended the same college several years later, the new focus was on dedicating oneself to full-time Christian ministry. Those who did the opposite of the prevailing ideal of the time generally experienced guilt at not pursuing what was considered to be more "spiritual."

Some people develop the mentality that if we don't help everyone in every situation at any time, we aren't good Christians. If we want to be more like Christ, we must continually and unconditionally give to others in need. Whenever asked, give. Wherever a need, fill it. Whoever is hurting, be there to soothe the pain. We needn't consult with God because we assume that we should offer assistance at all times, to all people, whenever asked. If we hesitate, guilt floods our souls. No wonder so many people experience codependency! When we begin to feel trapped and unappreciated, resentment corrodes our minds and guilt begins its downpour. Scripture *does* tell us to help those in need (the poor and afflicted), but I believe we should first seek God for wisdom and guidance lest we contribute to a codependent situation or rob someone else of the opportunity to give.

When I asked people about their God-related guilt feelings, they reported guilt . . .

☐ when I lie or swear, complain or gossip, lose self-control and get angry

---

☐ when I don't do my devotion or spend enough time in prayer

☐ when I miss the opportunity to tell a non-Christian about Jesus

---

☐ when I sin deliberately or disobey him

☐ when I think about sexual things

☐ when I do things my own way

☐ when I can't quit a bad habit

☐ when I read a novel instead of the Bible at times I've set aside for devotions

---

☐ when I spend money on things for myself

☐ when I fall asleep during prayer

Let's look at some of the ways guilt gets in the way of our understanding of God.

Fear Instead of Faith

Fear of God. Emphasizing God's displeasure at disobedience encourages a fearful rather than loving relationship with the Creator. When God is portrayed as the Great Punisher, we fall into fear. We then begin to view him as a dangerous predator rather than the loving Shepherd. Donald Sloat says, "The use of fear to motivate sensitive, vulnerable children toward the gospel is one of the most damaging methods used in the church, and in my estimation it has caused untold suffering among Christians, even causing many to flee the church and turn away from God."[4]

Several survey respondents wrote about the fear they experienced whenever they thought about God. Describing her religious upbringing, one person wrote, "I grew up afraid of God. The whole idea of God scared me. He was big and powerful and I was sinful and disobedient. They told us that he loved us, but all I can remember was stories about his anger at people's sins."

Fear of punishment. The fear of God and the fear of punishment go hand in hand. Comedian Flip Wilson used to say, "God'll get you for that!" It was a statement with which many people identified.

Many of us hold on to distorted perceptions of God as a God of wrath, punishment and fear. When we step out of line, even the slightest bit, we fear his retribution. When we stumble and fall, we expect a severe scolding. When we fall short, we wait for things to fall apart around us, indicating his displeasure. Many of us believe God primarily uses fear and guilt to motivate us. We mistakenly expect God to force, intimidate, punish, terrorize and harass us into obedience.

Thus we tend to believe in God more out of fear than out of faith. Our service is motivated more by duty than by love. We respond to God not out of worship but out of worry. When we view God in this way, our religion is held together by guilt and fear, not grace and love. One author writes,

> Because we're always aware that in many ways we fall short of what we should be as Christians, it's only natural to assume that God must be displeased with our performance. The more we let God down, the more we assume His anger, until such alienation sets into our minds that it is virtually impossible for us to enjoy a vital fellowship with God. And the pitiful tragedy is that all this is just in our minds. God isn't mad at us![5]

Fear of pleasure. Many years ago I joined the parachuting club at my college. I was quite excited about what I thought would be a thrill and a challenge. I remember choosing not to seek God's approval, though, because I assumed he would disapprove.

As the day drew near for my first jump, I decided that I'd better check in with him, since this was a dangerous endeavor. (I was motivated by fear of death, not obedience!) When I finally sought God in prayer, I learned several important truths.

I took a deep look at my perception of God. I realized I assumed that if I was to serve God wholeheartedly, he would require me to live an unexciting, dreary, dull and even miserable life. I knew my impression of him was wrong. God was not the "big tyrant in the sky" who wanted to make my life miserable and viewed all pleasure as detestable. He wanted me to be happy, to enjoy life, to obey him and to continually seek him for guidance. I had feared going to him in prayer because I thought he wouldn't want me to go ahead with my plan. But he isn't opposed to our pleasure and enjoyment as long as we let him be Lord of our lives.

Preaching on knowing God's will, a pastor said, "All too many Christians assume God's will is that we remain single, be poor and be called to be missionaries in a dreaded far-off country. Why? Because we think that being a dedicated, serious Christian means sacrificing what we enjoy and doing things we don't want to do." Such assumptions lead many of us to feel guilty whenever we experience pleasure.

> A child brought up in an environment . . . in which all worldly pleasures are frowned upon, will forswear dancing, flirtation, theatre-going, alcohol, tobacco, nice clothes, and any interest in good food. He will retain perhaps for the rest of his life the idea that everything pleasurable is forbidden, and a sin. . . . And so the Christian life appears to be for him an impoverishment, a dispossession, instead of a blossoming and a fulfillment.[6]

Unfortunately, many of us believe that if we are truly penitent we must forgo pleasure, for the Christian life is to be marked only by suffering and sacrifice. All pleasure and enjoyment are frivolous, irresponsible, undeserved—and therefore sinful. Marci confessed, "I feel guilty when something good happens to me. I have this idea that if I experience pleasure, it is sinful. It's hard to enjoy things, because I feel guilty if I do."

Legalism

> When I was growing up, the master list of forbidden things included tobacco in any form, alcohol, . . . dancing, bowling alleys, movies, cards, and, of course, such standard things as lying, stealing, and not going to church. Other sinful items included jewelry, flashy clothes, open-toed shoes for women, short hair for women, and so on. Television was often referred to as a "tool of hell."[7]

When our beliefs are based on rules, regulations and restrictions rather than a relationship with God, our faith will be empty. Rather than accept the totality of our sinful nature, we foolishly try to earn God's favor by adhering to a host of extrabiblical standards. We live by an elaborate list of dos and don'ts. Our focus shifts from God's grace to our deeds and behavior.

Many of us choose to respond this way because we don't like to feel that things are out of our hands. We want to be in control. By developing a comprehensive list of dos and don'ts, we are able to define what is appropriate and inappropriate behavior. We find comfort when guided by specific directions and clear-cut solutions. The authors of *Freedom from Guilt* write, "Although the Bible gives us guidelines, they are not enough for the insecure person. He cannot trust the internal guidance of the Holy Spirit, so he must seek detailed external rules to relieve his feelings of inadequacy. Legalistic rules fit right into our need for security."[8]

Unfortunately, this legalism is generally accompanied by hypocrisy, shallow faith and superficial façades. We become more concerned with appearances than our hidden faults, more concerned with what others think than what God desires. When this happens, "we hide our inner failures and hope God will give us credit for our outward actions. Thus we make legalistic rules a way of pulling the wool over our own eyes and of hiding from our own faults."[9]

We are not the only ones susceptible to this misguided way of thinking. The Bible has many examples of how the Pharisees attempted to use the law to achieve righteousness. They perpetuated the belief that strict adherence to the law was the way to be acceptable before God. Like the Pharisees, we establish a strict set of rules and regulations which we follow faithfully.

Legalism is enticing. It eases our guilty conscience because we feel that it lessens our sinfulness before God. It is much easier to follow a set of rules than to be left feeling defenseless. *But God wants our hearts more than our deeds, our praise more than our practices.*

The problem, of course, lies in the fact that there is absolutely nothing we can do to earn our salvation and to gain favor before God. It is a gift, neither earned nor deserved. No amount of work or adherence to rules and regulations will alter God's plan and perspective on who we are and how we are to be restored to relationship with him.

When we fall into the trap of believing that legalistic standards will cleanse us, we lose sight of the reason for Christ's atoning death. We begin to believe that our own behavior is what merits our acceptance by God. We deny the power of the cross and Jesus' atoning power. He already paid for our sin. He took away our guilt by his death at Calvary. Why insist on paying over and over again for an item that has already been purchased?

Bruce Narramore and Bill Counts write,

> Men seem to have an incurable bent toward legalism. . . . The basic reason, of course, lies in our rebelliousness toward God. We don't like to be told we can do absolutely nothing to merit his approval so we design a life-style that gives us at least a little credit for our actions. We are too proud to admit our total inability to please God, so we con ourselves into thinking that we can do at least a few acceptable things.[10]

Works, Not Faith

Another method of dealing with our sin is to try to earn God's favor through works on behalf of the kingdom. When we fall into this response, we find ourselves frantically doing "the Lord's work." We serve, volunteer, help, assist, make, lead, agree to, offer, give, accommodate, provide, consent and contribute whenever and wherever. Like those prone to legalism, we incorrectly believe that our actions and deeds will help change our "guilty" verdict and pay for our sin. We see these works as a sort of modern-day guilt offering. In Galatians 3:3, Paul points out the error: "Are you so foolish? After beginning with the Spirit, are you now trying to attain your goal by human effort?"

Self-Atonement

These responses are actually our feeble human attempts at self-atonement. We strive to earn our forgiveness, pay for our sins, make amends for our guilty nature and punish our deeds. When we deal with guilt through our works or through strict adherence to rules and regulations, through our actions or lifestyle, we mistakenly return to a "salvation by works" mentality. We believe that *our* actions, deeds and behaviors make us okay before God—reducing the devastating impact of our sin, somehow making us more presentable.

It's hard for us to accept the fact that God's gift of forgiveness is free. We can do nothing to earn it or to pay for it.

Religion and Guilt Go Together When . . .

Guilt accompanies religion when we lead a legalistic life or fall into the grip of the fears mentioned previously. When our faith *produces* rather than *reduces* guilt, we have allowed a distorted view of God to infiltrate our beliefs. This can happen in the following ways.

Religion brings guilt through
- ☐ distorted views of God
- ☐ fear of punishment
- ☐ fear of pleasure
- ☐ legalism

Religion brings guilt when we view God as a God of
- ☐ rules, rituals and regulations
- ☐ retribution and retaliation
- ☐ rebukes and reprimands
- ☐ reproach and restrictions

When we are exposed to such distorted views of our faith and of God, we invite guilt to set up permanent residence in our hearts. If our faith is based on fear, our relationship with God will lack depth and we will live shallow Christian lives, retreating behind religious façades. When this happens, our faith becomes a farce and hypocrisy sets in.

Michel de Montaigne said, "I find no quality so easy to counterfeit as religious devotion." On the outside we pretend to believe while feeling overwhelmed with doubt, fear and guilt on the inside. Like the little pig's house of straw, our fear-based, shallow, distorted religion will fall easily—and guilt is the big bad wolf that comes and blows it down.

We should experience guilt in relation to *our* sin, not in relation to *God's* character. He is a God of love, mercy, grace and forgiveness, not of reproach and rebukes. He is the One who made a way for the cleansing of our guilt through the atoning blood of Jesus Christ. *God doesn't want to add to our guilt—he wants to take our guilt away.*

Application Questions

1. How do you view God—as a tyrant, an ogre, an easily displeased drill sergeant? Are you hanging on to some distorted views of God?

2. Is your faith motivated by fear of punishment or disapproval? Are you caught up in legalistic rules and regulations?

3. Did you identify with the pastor's comment that many Christians believe that to be truly dedicated you must forgo anything pleasurable?

4. Does your faith produce or reduce guilt?

Prayer

Lord, please deliver us from our distorted views of you. Help us to see you for who you are—the majestic Lord of the universe and loving Savior. Amen.

EIGHT

Expectations, Culture & Guilt

*L*uci came for counseling because she didn't like herself and continually felt like a failure. Luci was in her early thirties, employed and living at home with her widowed mother. She expressed a desire to be more independent. Her mother constantly told her that if she was a good daughter she'd stay at home and help her. Luci struggled with a deep sense of guilt at not wanting to continue living at home, not doing everything her mother wanted and not being the "perfect" daughter. Trying to live up to her mother's expectations made her miserable.

Expectations, whether from others or from ourselves, can challenge or convict us, exhilarate or exhaust us. They can lead us to greater heights as we seek to fulfill them, or they can lead to the depths of despair as we fall under their enormous weight.

Our behavior is largely determined by the expectations placed on us by others, be they family, friends, bosses, pastors, coworkers, the media, advertisements, institutions or societal codes of behavior. These expectations motivate much of what we do and don't do. Many of us govern our lives by what others think, promote or expect. When we fail to meet up to the expectations of others, guilt usually comes flooding in. And our own expectations can be just as damaging, punitive and guilt-producing as those projected onto us by others.

"Guilt is often tied to rigorous, perfectionist standards. People want to be something they cannot be or to satisfy others' expectations which cannot be satisfied, and their dilemma results in thoughts and feelings which cannot be distinguished from guilt."[1] *Unmet expectations are often accompanied by feelings of frustration, failure and guilt.*

The Power of Expectations

Social scientists tell us that our desires to belong and to feel worthwhile and competent are among our strongest human needs. We desire to meet others' expectations and to please them because we want to feel connected and gain approval and don't want to be viewed as incompetent. *If we fail to meet others' expectations, we fear rejection, abandonment and loneliness.*

In order to subdue these fears we often compromise who we are. We seek to meet others' expectations at all costs. In some cases the price is high. When we succumb to expectations, we may become dependent on others to guide and direct our lives. We may lose sight of who we are and what we value as we focus our energies on others' desires for us. We may become passive and nonassertive, a pleaser or a chameleon, becoming a different person in different situations with different people.

The sacrifices we make in order to meet others' expectations are more costly than they are worth when our fears cause us to compromise who we are. We may feel guilty when we are unable to live up to others' expectations, and we may feel guilty for compromising who we are in order to please others. It seems that guilt gets us either way!

Others' Expectations

A study conducted to examine various emotions found that the most common source of guilt is other people. We feel guilty if we disappoint others, let them down or don't live up to their expectations. These who shape and affect our lives so profoundly with their subtle or not-so-subtle expectations can be our parents, extended family, teachers, coaches, coworkers, supervisors and friends—even bus drivers, post office employees and bank tellers.

Some of us feel guilty if the store clerk gives us a look of disgust, if the driver behind us acts impatient or if the newspaper deliverer is perturbed because we don't have the exact change. We feel guilty if our parents expect us to visit, our friends expect us to call or our families expect us to spend more time together.

One person summed it up with strong words: "I feel *horribly* guilty when I let someone down or don't meet the expectations someone has for me, so I often try harder to do what is expected." When we try harder and harder to meet others' expectations we sink into a bottomless pit, because it is impossible to meet everyone's standards. When we try to be all things to all people, we inevitably fail and end up feeling guilty.

Parental expectations. Our parents' expectations generally have the strongest pull, because we encountered them daily while growing up. While many of their expectations were spoken, others went unspoken but were nonetheless clearly understood. The expectations reflected their desires and hopes for our future, our behavior, grades, associates, interests and skills. They had a strong say in what they thought was right for us. Some of their expectations were realistic, applicable and wise. Some were not. Their voiced and unvoiced beliefs about what was best for us were at times merely reflections of their own needs and wants. While their intentions were generally more admirable than abominable, we were still left trying to fulfill their every expectation—to please them.

We carry many of our parents' expectations with us into adulthood. Rather than unshackle ourselves from the grip of their unrealistic or inapplicable expectations, we continue to walk as if weighed down by a ball and chain. Do we really expect to continue to fulfill their expectations? When do we grow up and grow away from their harmful hopes? When do we free ourselves from the self-imposed prison of parental expectations?

One man feels alienated and guilty because he didn't pursue the career his parents expected. One family plans all vacations around visits to the in-laws because it is expected. Young couples begin having children earlier than planned because of parental pestering. Some seek job advancements because of parental pressure. Many people make phone calls out of obligation, not desire.

We will never live up to all of our parents' expectations, no matter how hard we try and no matter how long we keep trying. Some of their expectations serve to prod us on to greater heights, challenging us to be all that we can be. Others only stifle our growth as we try and fail to meet them. Some of the expectations our parents have or had for us need to be destroyed so that they will stop stalking us.

Luci came to understand that her mother's expectations were unhealthy and self-serving. As she let go of her feelings of obligation to please her mother, her self-esteem increased. She continued to express love and concern for her mother but slowly began to let go of the burden of trying to meet her mother's excessive and demanding expectations—and to live free from that excessive guilt.

Significant others' expectations. But parents aren't the only ones whose expectations have had an impact on our lives. Coaches, music teachers, youth leaders and others also contributed to our developing self-esteem. Their encouragement warmed our souls, and their discouragement chilled our hearts. We wanted to please them and to emulate their every move. We wanted to succeed in order to gain their approval or avoid their disapproval. We craved their attention and cowered at their disappointment.

These significant people played an important role in forming who we are today. If most of their expectations were positive, we were spurred on to face greater challenges. If most of their expectations seemed unattainable, they brought conviction rather than challenge. Rather than "Good job!" we got guilt. Due to their prominent position in our formative years, we were often left feeling inadequate. These many people negatively and positively affected us with their expectations—expectations that continue to affect us, our self-esteem and our sense of guilt even into adulthood.

Self-Expectations
Our own expectations are the goals, hopes and aspirations we have for ourselves. They should be realistic, attainable and applicable to us and our situation. Guilt sets in when we develop expectations that are impossible to attain. When expectations are unmet, it is usually be-

cause they are unrealistic or inapplicable. *Unrealistic* expectations are too lofty and unattainable. They immobilize us rather than motivate us. *Inapplicable* expectations simply don't apply to us—they're inappropriate. They may be attainable and realistic for someone else, but when applied to us and our particular situation, personality and interests, the shoe doesn't fit. Unfortunately, like Cinderella's stepsisters, too many of us keep trying to stuff our foot into a shoe that was never meant to fit.

Joel Wells writes, "Far more serious and far more fertile sources of contemporary guilt feelings reside in our acquired self-expectations, over-inflated sense of responsibility, ambition, and the notion that we must not only be perfect but be all things to all people."[2] Many of us have overinflated expectations that need to be brought down to size.

It's okay to want to excel and do the best we can, but to expect ourselves to be *the* best or to be "perfect" in all we do is unrealistic and unreasonable. Our perfectionistic tendencies usually spill over to those around us. We often find ourselves feeling guilty when our families, relationships and work don't meet up to our standards and expectations.

One author writes, "It is not noble to want perfection; it is cruel. We could spend the rest of our lives feeling guilt—or we can accept our imperfections as part of what is real."[3] *Expectations should be healthy and harm-free.*

We also invite guilt when we develop our expectations by comparing ourselves to others. Of course there will always be someone who is better at something than we are. Comparing ourselves to others generally leaves us feeling inadequate and guilty every time we don't measure up. Our self-expectations should reflect our aspirations without exasperating us. They should spur us on to meet new challenges rather than overwhelm us. It's like mountain climbing: if the peak is too steep and too far away, we run the risk of not being able to reach it.

Let's abolish our futile attempts at perfection. Let's abandon the tendency to compare ourselves with others. Let's get rid of our unrealistic, unattainable, inapplicable and impossible expectations and replace them with realistic, challenging, attainable and God-inspired ones.

Cultural Expectations

Society's idea of "perfect" and other cultural expectations are also significant contributors to many of our unnecessary guilt feelings. Society's messages often undermine our feelings of accomplishment and are detrimental to the development of our self-acceptance. The messages are both direct and indirect. The media, movies, television programs and advertisements tell us what clothes, styles and colors are "in," what recreational activities and possessions are "must haves," what lifestyle is preferred, what car and food we "deserve" and what vacation we "owe" ourselves. Society and the media tell us what is currently acceptable and appropriate and what's not. When we feel that we don't fit in or aren't what we should be according to society and the media, guilt gets us.

The problem is that society's opinions and popular fads may come and go. Even many research studies seem to contradict or later disprove one another. Let's examine some of the main areas that can be guilt-producing.

Advertising guilt. Advertising's job is to sell products and services. The tactics advertisers use are persuasive, attempting to create a need or a desire within us that can be satisfied only when we purchase their particular product. Millions of dollars are spent on marketing research to determine how to induce guilt, fear or a sense of inadequacy in order to seduce us into buying certain products.

One ad insinuates that if we *really* love our children, we will buy a certain brand of sugary breakfast cereal. Another ad tells us that if we *really* care about our children, we will restrict their sugar intake and use a particular brand of toothpaste. Telephone ads tell us that if we *really* love someone, we will call them more often. We are told to buy diamonds, send flowers and cards and buy all the latest toys, clothes and games for those we love. If we don't buy *this* fire alarm, our family will die. If we don't buy *this* insurance, our family will experience hardship when we have a prolonged hospital stay. If we don't buy *this* product, we will be less desirable.

Advertisements imply that we are "out of it," insensitive, uncaring or stupid without their product. Perhaps this seems overstated, but the fact is many of us are left feeling guilty, fearful and incomplete if we don't consume advertised goods.

Each guilt-producing ad should be required to carry a warning: "Caution: This advertisement may be dangerous to your mental health." [Advertising has] probably made you more self-conscious about your body and more insecure about your appearance and the appearance of your home, as well as your role and your lifestyle. It may frequently make you feel inadequate. . . . Most likely, it makes you feel guilty at times because you can't do, buy or be all that you see.[4]

Lifestyle guilt. Our society and the media presume to inform us about how we should live our lives. Television taunts us with the lives of the rich and famous, with information about how to get rich quick and how to spend our money. These perspectives have contributed to the development of unrealistic lifestyle expectations. People begin to believe falsely that money and materialism bring happiness.

Richard Foster admonishes us,

Because we lack a divine Center our need for security has led us into an insane attachment to things. We must clearly understand that the lust for affluence in contemporary society is psychotic. It is psychotic because it has completely lost touch with reality. We crave things we neither need nor enjoy. . . . It is time we awaken to the fact that conformity to a sick society is to be sick.[5]

We live in a society that is impatient with delays. We expect instant success, drive-through happiness and quick-fix solutions to our problems. Advertisements that portray this immediate-fix mentality lead us to believe that we should expect it.

The influence of the prevailing culture pulls us toward unhealthy expectations. If life doesn't go as planned, many of us tend to blame ourselves rather than the society that has set up unrealistic standards. When a certain brand of mouthwash doesn't improve our social life as promised, many of us question ourselves rather than the product's advertising gimmick.

Food guilt. My salad dressing, which is fat free, says I can now eat without feeling guilty. A national frozen-yogurt chain encourages consumption of its product because we can enjoy it guiltlessly. Ads for a new brand of potato chips state that they are guiltless. While these products encourage freedom from guilt, one advertisement for ice cream tells us to "enjoy the guilt." Guilt and food often go together.

For some, eating compulsions are real and can be traumatizing. Diet becomes the focus of much time and energy. But for most of us, eating is something we enjoy—depending on the amount of guilt we experience.

Fifteen years ago I didn't feel guilty about eating foods high in fat. In fact, I enjoyed them—delicious pastries full of luscious butter, barbecued spare ribs dripping with fat, real ice cream. Back then our society wasn't as concerned about the dietary problems of high fat as it is today. It has only been in recent years that fat has been pronounced a dietary outlaw. It is to be avoided, replaced and whenever possible abandoned.

A diabetic friend feels guilty when she indulges in desserts because her health is at risk. Another friend, nondiabetic, also feels flooded with guilt after consuming sweets because "I should watch my weight." A skinny person told me that he feels guilty eating in front of dieting friends. When I saw our family physician at the grocery store, she felt guilty for having pork ribs in her cart. "Don't look," she said. "I know they're unhealthy."

When people were asked about food guilt, they responded,

☐ I feel guilty when I eat too much junk food or chocolate or foods high in cholesterol and fat.

☐ I feel guilty when I overeat or eat when I'm not hungry.

☐ I feel guilty because I should lose weight.

☐ I feel guilty because I eat when I'm feeling frustrated and lonely.

What we do and don't eat can be a source of a variety of guilt feelings. If one has dietary concerns or health risks, is pregnant or has another condition that dictates a specific diet, guilt feelings can serve a good purpose. However, if we eat to fill an emotional void, we should seek assistance to help us understand and change these patterns. Feeling guilty in these situations may be an incentive for positive change. But if we don't have dietary or health restrictions, being overcome with guilt for everything we eat and don't eat is counterproductive. We should strive for good nutrition, but flogging ourselves with the guilt whip usually doesn't help.

Fitness guilt. The President's Council on Physical Fitness was formed many years ago in an attempt to increase the physical well-being of American citizens. North Americans soon became overwhelmed with a new area of inadequacy. Those who didn't get with the program were derogatorily labeled "couch potatoes" and became outcasts in this new social order esteeming the physically fit.

While I *firmly* agree with the benefits of healthy, fit bodies, I don't agree that this preferred status should be accompanied by an overwhelming sense of guilt for those who don't *fit* the ideal (pun intended). The media don't show us average people, only superjocks. Many people give up exercise before getting started because the ideal seems out of reach. As a result, there are many people who feel frustrated, embarrassed or guilty about being out of shape.

When I asked people what they felt guilty about regarding exercise, I realized that for many, exercising is a no-win situation. Those who do exercise said they feel guilty because it takes too much time away from important relationships, because they're inconsistent, because they don't enjoy it and because "enough is never enough." Those who don't exercise are visited by guilt because they feel neglectful, lazy and dissatisfied. Guilty if we do, guilty if we don't.

Weight guilt. In ancient Rome, being thin was considered repulsive, and those who were plump were deemed attractive. Fat was in and thin was out. Today our society transmits unending messages declaring that thin is in. Many of us are overly concerned and obsessed with our weight. Diet centers are swamped with people who feel guilty about their weight. Perhaps we need more self-acceptance and less emphasis on weight.

A research study measuring women's self-esteem asked participants to rate themselves in several areas before and after reading several popular women's magazines. Results indicated that women's opinions of themselves lowered after having been exposed to the magazines. The researchers found that most articles and advertisements focused on the perfect body, unblemished skin, impeccable clothes and ideal sex. To most of us, these seem unattainable.

Society's Message Versus God's Message

Society and the media convey the simple message that we must conform to their image of what's right, what's in and what's acceptable. Our standards, however, should be set by God, not the prevailing culture. We need to hear his voice amidst the cultural clamor. Pope

John Paul II warned us when he wrote, "The media have conditioned society to listen to what it wants it to hear."[6]

The Bible does tell us that we are to take care of our bodies, for they are "the temple of the Holy Spirit" (1 Cor 6:19-20). We are told to avoid gluttony (Prov 23:20-21). We are taught to be concerned about what we eat when it might cause another to stumble (Rom 14:20-21; 1 Cor 8:13). And we are admonished not to be lazy (Prov 10:4; Heb 6:12). But God's Word also admonishes us, "Do not love the world or anything in the world. If anyone loves the world, the love of the Father is not in him. For everything in the world—the cravings of sinful man, the lust of his eyes and the boasting of what he has and does—comes not from the Father but from the world" (1 Jn 2:15-16). First Peter 2:11 reminds us that we are "aliens and strangers in the world."

God wants us to be *in* this world but not *of* this world. He wants to be the One who determines what is true, noble, right, pure, lovely, admirable, excellent and praiseworthy (Phil 4:8). These are the things he wants us to focus on. We must make sure that we pursue his priorities, not those of the prevailing culture.

God's Expectations

When expectations overwhelm us, whether from others, ourselves or our culture, we are less able to discern what God expects of us. Chasing after inappropriate expectations distracts us from God because our energy is spent trying to fulfill impossible dreams.

The more we free ourselves from the inapplicable expectations of others and the unrealistic expectations we impose on ourselves, the more we are able to experience the inner peace and abundant life our Lord offers. It is a snare to fear others' opinions, "but whoever trusts in the LORD is kept safe" (Prov 29:25). Fearing what others think ensnares and enslaves us, but trusting in God keeps us safe and free.

Trying to fulfill unrealistic expectations results in failure, frustration, guilt and low self-esteem. When we reject them, we are free to pursue God's desires for us. Realistic expectations help us to grow personally and spiritually. When we fulfill them, our self-esteem increases, and we are better able to do and be what God wants.

Minimizing Guilt and Maximizing God-Guided Expectations

Here are some suggestions on how to develop realistic expectations and get rid of the guilt-producing ones:

☐ Accept our strengths *and* weaknesses/limitations

☐ Expect to do *our* best rather than be *the* best

☐ Forgive ourselves for past mistakes and unfulfilled expectations

☐ Discard others' unrealistic or inapplicable expectations (whether from people, the media or society)

☐ Don't compare ourselves to others or expect perfection

☐ Discern what we value and esteem (rather than be overly influenced by cultural expectations and others' opinions)

☐ Seek to know God and his expectations

As we attempt to rid ourselves of the expectations that hinder our emotional and spiritual well-being, we must look to God for insight and guidance. Proverbs 3:5-6 encourages us to lean on him and not on our own understanding. To know his expectations is to know he who is both the God of the universe and the God of our hearts. His expectations are love-motivated, freeing, encouraging and realistic. He loves and knows us completely and wants the best for us. As we read his Word, pray and are still before him, we increase our ability to be guided by his Spirit and not our own.

Application Questions

1. In what specific ways do you experience guilt with regard to your lifestyle, exercise, food and weight?

2. The apostle Paul advises us, "Do not conform any longer to the pattern of this world, but be transformed by the renewing of your mind. Then you will be able to test and approve what God's will is—his good, pleasing and perfect will" (Rom 12:2). What does it mean to be conformed to this world?

3. Read 1 Corinthians 6:19-20: "Do you not know that your body is a temple of the Holy Spirit, who is in you, whom you have received from God? You are not your own; you were bought at a price. Therefore honor God with your body." Explain what Paul is saying.

4. What does it mean to be "*in* this world but not *of* this world"? What can we gain from 2 Corinthians 1:12: "Now this is our boast: Our conscience testifies that we have conducted ourselves in the world. . . . We have done so not according to worldly wisdom but according to God's grace"?

5. Have you fallen into some unhealthy patterns of trying to meet others' expectations?

6. How can you lessen the amount of influence and control others' expec-

tations have on your daily decisions while increasing your ability to be led by the Spirit of God?

7. How can you make self-expectations more realistic so that unnecessary guilt doesn't pay a visit?

Prayer

Lord, please help us to be in this world but not of this world, to not be conformed to the standards and values of our culture and times. We desire that our lives honor you and that the expectations we seek to fulfill are those given in your Word and by your will. Thank you. Amen.

N I N E

Guilt-Ridden Masks

Susan wanted to attend a conference because she felt it could be instrumental to her professional development and perhaps lead to better job opportunities and an increase in salary. However, she knew that the time away from both work and family would be a financial as well as emotional hardship on her husband. The longer she thought about her desire to attend the conference, the more her feelings of guilt developed. While part of her argued that her attendance would benefit the family in the long run, she continued to struggle with the imposed inconvenience.

As the guilt feelings grew, she found herself feeling angry at her husband and family, resentful for her lack of freedom and what she perceived as her husband's unreasonable demands. Although he had voiced his consent, she decided that it must not have been sincere.

As the conference neared and Susan's guilt feelings increased, she blew up in anger. "I don't think I'm being selfish in wanting to go to this conference. I think it's important, and I don't understand why you aren't supporting me in this decision. My absence will be a minor inconvenience, not a major catastrophe!" Her husband, of course, was dumbfounded and surprised, not knowing why he was the target of this outburst.

Jim was a junior partner in a growing accounting firm. His future looked promising. His encounters with the senior partners, however, had often left him somewhat uncomfortable. He dismissed it, telling himself, *I just don't know the whole picture. It's probably nothing.* After each meeting with the partners, his understanding of the whole picture grew, as did his level of discomfort. He discovered that the firm continually listed several expenses as tax deductible which were not legally considered such, both in the business's own operation and in the accounting of certain clients. He knew that these practices were unethical, yet he didn't want to lose the security of his position and prospects with the firm.

In an effort to resolve his uneasiness, Jim began telling himself, *That's the way it's done in our profession. The ethical guidelines are too restrictive and don't take into account the day-to-day implementation of the business.* As time progressed, Jim's feelings of guilt subsided, and he began participating in the unethical practices.

The Great Guilt Cover-Up
When a driver honked at me the other day, I got angry. My thoughts focused on his rude, unnecessary action. Later that afternoon, as I was thinking about this book, the driving incident came to mind. I realized that my gut feeling was not really anger but guilt. It was the other driver who had a right to be angry, not me. While attempting a left-hand turn onto a major street, I had pulled out too far and blocked the intersection. I didn't have the right of way and was creating a potentially dangerous situation. My feelings of anger were actually rooted in guilt.

The more I examine my own feelings and motives and those of the people I see in counseling, the more I've come to realize that *many of the emotions we experience are rooted in guilt.* Those feelings that we readily identify are often not the primary, motivating emotion. Anger, discouragement, jealousy, apathy and fear, among others, are often secondary emotions to guilt.

We become experts at covering up, ignoring and blinding ourselves to our true inner sense of guilt. Why? Because for many of us, they are less desirable and less recognizable than other emotional responses. We mask our guilt feelings with other responses and feelings. *This is the great guilt cover-up.*

Susan and Jim illustrate some of these cover-ups. Their responses resulted from their inability to recognize the guilt-root of their feelings. Guilt feelings were considered uncomfortable, undesirable or unacceptable, so their personal defense mechanisms kicked in and sought ways to cover them up.

We human beings find guilt distasteful. We don't want to face it, so we create masks or ways to cover it up. In *The Scarlet Letter,* Nathaniel Hawthorne wrote, "No man, for any considerable period, can wear one face to himself, and another to the multitude, without finally getting bewildered as to which may be the true." Our guilt masks become so automatic that they are often difficult to detect. We become experts at this great guilt cover-up. Before we have the opportunity to initiate an appropriate response, our defense mechanisms have already gone into action.

Unfaced guilt is the great blackmailer. The victim hides his failures by putting on a brave face to the world. But he is pressured in myriad ways to make the payments to guarantee that his secret will not be revealed. The psychic resources of the victim are being constantly depleted and the best aspects of the human experience are extorted from him. No matter how great his material wealth, he lives in psychic squalor and poverty.[1]

The Guilt Trap

When we feel vulnerable or threatened, our defense mechanisms function to protect us. While they can be helpful in many situations, they can be detrimental when it comes to guilt. When our guilt feelings are due to an actual sin, these defenses might keep us from turning to God. On the other hand, if we are experiencing bad guilt, the defensive strategies might keep us from exposing the falsehood of that guilt.

Our defense mechanisms act like an outer protective layer. If we discover that these temporary defenses are inadequate to safeguard us from the onslaught of guilt, we fortify ourselves by developing additional layers. Figure 1 illustrates this.

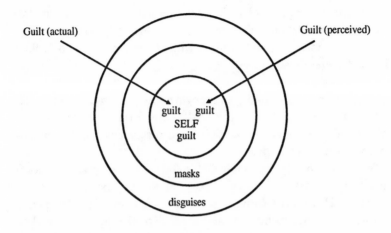

Figure 1

The first layer that surrounds us represents the temporary masks we use to protect ourselves from facing guilt. When they become ineffective, another layer develops to help fortify our defenses against guilt. The further we get from the inner circle, which represents our feelings and thoughts, the further we are from being able to deal with guilt.

The irony is that *while we think we are keeping guilt out, we are actually trapping it inside.* We think we are setting up a quarantine so that guilt won't spread. In reality, however, we are allowing it to fester inside like a deadly infection. This fortification of guilt is self-destructive. While we think we are keeping it out, we are only keeping it from showing.

These layers we build to protect ourselves actually prevent us from facing guilt.

How do *you* deal with feelings of guilt?

☐ Do you constantly analyze them, or do you have difficulty identifying them for what they are?

☐ Do you ignore them, pretending they don't exist?

☐ Do you get angry at others or yourself?

☐ Do you repent and ask forgiveness over and over and over again?

☐ Do you become discouraged and downtrodden?

☐ Do you avoid people, places or things that remind you of the guilt feelings?

☐ Do you develop headaches, lose your concentration or blame others?

☐ How *do* you deal with guilt feelings?

We will identify five types of masks: physical, social, behavioral, mental and emotional, and spiritual. As we lower our defenses and remove the masks, we will be able to deal with guilt face to face.

Physical Masks

June's baby was born with Down syndrome. Though there were no complications with the birthing process or with postpartum recovery, June soon began experiencing severe headaches. She assumed that they were related to a physical problem, not an emotional one. Similarly, Dave developed ulcers shortly after he'd been involved in a car accident where one of the members of his carpool was killed.

For many people, unwanted feelings and experiences get translated into physical ailments. Those in the medical profession have become increasingly aware of the connection between negative emotional experiences and various health problems. Someone once said, "Our bodies are not meant to carry what our emotions are meant to express." Guilt feelings are no exception.

For many, feelings of guilt manifest themselves physically with neck and backaches, sweaty hands, increased perspiration, tense muscles, ⟵ upset stomach, indigestion, ulcers, headaches and other symptoms. Dave's and June's situations illustrate this. The guilt feelings after the accident and the baby's birth turned inward and manifested themselves physically.

Guilt that has not been dealt with effectively may rob us of our ⟵ physical strength and stamina, increasing our susceptibility to illness. If we are experiencing physical symptoms without an apparent physical cause, then perhaps we need to ask ourselves if guilt is hiding somewhere inside.

Social Masks

When we are plagued with guilt, our relationships are affected. We may deal with our guilt feelings by *withdrawing* socially. Perhaps we feel that everyone can read our hearts and minds and know the ugliness within. So we stay away from people for fear of being exposed. We interact less and less with others because of our feelings of guilt and shame.

When Gary missed an important deadline at work, his boss was understanding and extended the deadline a few days. But even though Gary finished the project according to the new schedule, he was overcome by guilt feelings. He began *avoiding* his boss because the guilt feelings would emerge in great strength every time he saw him. Gary subconsciously implemented the "out of sight, out of mind" defense; the less he saw of his boss, the less guilt he felt. He began to enjoy his work less and less and eventually started looking for another job. His guilt feelings came between him and his boss, alienating the relationship and ultimately affecting his work morale.

We avoid people who arouse guilt feelings. If we haven't contacted a friend as expected, we avoid places where we might run into her. If we didn't keep a promise, we avoid the people affected by our transgression. If we feel guilty for being busy outside the home, we may continue to stay away because guilt stabs our hearts whenever we go home. *Unresolved guilt feelings can act as a forceful wedge in ruining relationships.*

For some of us, guilt feelings increase our desire to find others with similar flaws. Locating other "fallen" or guilt-ridden individuals helps ease our conscience and discomfort. We focus on others' problems and don't deal with our own. *Uncovering others' faults* in an effort to soothe our own sense of guilt and imperfection doesn't help. In fact it often makes it worse, because our own problems don't go away when we concentrate on others' predicaments. We also become easily tempted to gossip.

Perhaps this is why we as a society are so fascinated with hearing of others' downfalls and why tabloids, soap operas and headlines about fallen stars are so appealing. Fault-finding and gossip are tempting because they help us to feel better about our own situation in several ways:

1. We feel a sense of superiority over those whose misdeeds and calamities are exposed.

2. We realize we are not alone in our wretchedness.

3. We focus on others' faults and not our own.

4. It gives us something to blame—society and its ills, our culture, the president, our educational system and so on.

Behavioral Masks and Changes

Rick decided that his son should earn half of the money needed to buy the new baseball glove he wanted. He felt it would help in teaching him financial responsibility. But when Rick forgot his son's baseball game one day, he went out and bought the glove because he felt guilty. By doing so he deprived his son of the opportunity to learn about saving money.

When Rick bought the baseball glove for his son, he was seeking to *compensate* for his guilt feelings. He hoped that his action would lessen the guilt he was experiencing. We may compensate by giving extra money to a charitable cause, saying extra prayers, walking an extra mile, giving gifts and flowers or volunteering. We respond to our feelings of guilt by doing things to *appease* our guilt or compensate for it. Our normal good sense may be temporarily out of order because we are obsessed with getting rid of the guilt feelings that are plaguing us.

Sometimes when I'm feeling guilty about something my *behavior changes.* I may become more talkative (which is a nervous, self-conscious response to my guilt feelings). At other times I turn inward and become introspective and quiet. These changes tell me that something is going on inside that needs to be addressed.

When overcome by pervasive guilt feelings we may *act in ways that seem out of the ordinary* or unusual for our personality. A normally shy, quiet person may become more talkative and outgoing, an extrovert more introverted, a calm person more easily stressed. Those who are meticulous may become careless, and the graceful may become clumsy. A reserved person may become more obnoxious, a conservative person liberal, a modest person flamboyant, a selfless person more hedonistic. These behavioral changes may be momentary masks or permanent disguises. They may reflect an evening of mischief or a brief pose.

There also may be times when we *act out or behave inappropriately* because we are unable to sort through what we are feeling. When children experience unwanted feelings, they often act out in defiance or disobedience because they have not learned how to verbalize their frustrations or deal with their emotions. Once we become adults this problem doesn't automatically go away. The deep, unwanted feelings we are experiencing may emerge in ways that are harmful or irresponsible. We may physically strike out at a person or an object (assault, vandalism), we may act inappropriately in certain social settings (loud verbal abuse), or we may not fulfill a commitment. We act in ways that we normally detest.

Guilt may also lead us to engage in *self-destructive behavior*. When we consciously or subconsciously do things that have the potential to harm us, we may be acting out a need to punish ourselves for some actual or perceived sin. The self-destructive behavior may be a slow, ongoing neglect of our health, an evening of reckless risks and daring deeds, or self-mutilation.

Mental and Emotional Masks
Some of us deal with unwanted guilt feelings by becoming more emotional (agitated, teary, aggressive, depressed). Others become more affected mentally (forgetful, unable to concentrate, confused). Those highlighted in this section are but a few of the many ways we mask guilt's appearance.

Guilt feelings can undergo a *transformation* and come out as another emotion. Susan, who wanted to attend a professional conference, transformed her feelings of guilt into anger. Her guilt was perhaps too painful, uncomfortable or unrecognizable, so she transformed it. By turning the guilt into anger and directing it outward, she was able to relieve her anxiety.

When I became irritated at the other driver, like Susan I transformed my guilt into anger. While I thought I was mad at the driver, I was actually feeling guilty about what I'd done. When we exchange guilt for anger, someone suffers. Either we turn our anger outward, directing it at innocent others, or we focus the anger at ourselves. Susan's guilt-motivated anger got displaced onto her husband. She directed her anger outward in an act of self-preservation. Many of us find it easier and safer to redirect our anger inward. When our anger focuses inward, we may become depressed or experience physical problems. When our anger focuses outward, we project blame onto others and end up with wounded relationships.

When guilt is transformed into another emotion such as anger, it is more difficult to deal with and detect. We put a protective shield around the guilt to prevent it from being exposed.

Guilt is also frequently transformed into *pride or selfishness.* Jim, the junior accountant, could easily have turned the guilt he was feeling into pride. He could have told himself, *I know better than those who set up the ethical standards of our profession what is best in practice. They probably only dealt with theory—I deal with reality.* He could have become prideful in order to cover up the unwanted feelings within. Wanting to go to the conference, Susan could have allowed her guilt to become selfishness: "I'll do whatever I want whenever I want." She could have stuffed guilt in the closet and decided to wear selfish attire instead.

For many, guilt feelings are transformed into an overall feeling of *Who cares?* or *So what?* When we are unable to overcome discouragement, *apathy* takes over. Our ability to defeat unnecessary guilt vanishes and is replaced by a sense of helplessness and hopelessness. We plod along each day without taking a look at the true source of the apathy because it drains our emotional resources. It becomes so pervasive that we no longer have the strength to unearth the root of the problem—guilt.

Another useful mask we wear in our efforts to avoid facing guilt is *self-condemnation and pity.* Karen constantly told herself, *I should be a better mom.* Whenever she disciplined her children, she struggled with whether she had been too severe or too lenient. She questioned if she was doing the right thing and was constantly overcome with guilt feelings.

Karen condemned herself because she felt she should be a better mother. Her guilt led her down a path of discouragement and despair. Whether the guilt was justified or not (good guilt or bad guilt), she became self-deprecating and full of doubt, self-conscious rather than self-confident.

Self-condemnation often leads to self-pity. By feeling sorry for ourselves, we draw attention away from our guilt. We soon forget what caused the "pity party" and settle in to enjoy the festivities. Condemning ourselves, we begin to feel better because we are receiving self-imposed chastening for our perceived misdeed.

When Mary forgot to visit her mother as planned, she immediately told herself, *I can't do anything right. Why do I even try? I'm a terrible daughter.* It didn't matter whether her mother was understanding. Self-condemnation overpowers our ability to sort out unwanted feelings and behaviors and becomes the center of attention. Though guilt is the root, we see only the overgrown weed of self-criticism.

Another common guilt cover-up occurs when we take our negative feelings and place them onto another (called *projection*). Susan illustrated this when she projected her negative (guilt) feelings onto her unsuspecting husband. We dislike guilt so much that we try to pass it on to others, generally in ways that are manipulative and destructive.

Even in the Garden of Eden, Adam neglected to take responsibility for his actions by blaming his misdeeds on Eve—and even God. In a sense, he said, "It's your fault, God, not mine, because it was you who gave me the woman." Eve, in turn, blamed the serpent rather than admit her disobedience (Gen 3:11-13). Albert Camus, a famous French philosopher, novelist, playwright and journalist, stated it well when he wrote in his novel *The Fall:* "Each man insists on being innocent, even if it means accusing the whole human race, and heaven."

When we project our blame onto others, we are sending them on a guilt trip meant for us. Whenever we hurl anger or accusations at another person without first examining the basis of our feelings, we are endangering the relationship. We are often too quick to accuse others before examining our own culpability. Blame projection is a costly mask to wear.

Another guilt-hiding technique is *minimizing.* "It's not that big a deal." "Don't worry about it—it's nothing." "Let's not make a mountain out of a molehill." At first Jim, the accountant, dealt with his guilt feelings by minimizing the importance of the situation, telling himself, *It's probably nothing.* If he were to acknowledge the depth of the problem, the guilt feelings might be too overwhelming. It's easier to minimize the impact and importance of the problem than to come face to face with guilt.

We minimize our infractions as well as our feelings. We make our sins smaller and our guilt slighter. We try to convince ourselves that they are only a kitty cat instead of a roaring lion.

Joe offered to help during a special cleanup day at the church. He knew that there was a lot to do and few workers. When the day came, though, Joe really wanted to watch a football game on television. In his efforts to soothe his guilt, Joe told himself, *They probably didn't need me anyway. I wouldn't have been much help with my bad back. There really wasn't too much to do.* Joe's response illustrates our keen human ability to *rationalize* our behaviors. We rationalize our actions by telling ourselves, *It was for the best, It wouldn't have worked out anyway* or *They deserved what they got.*

The author of *Integrity Therapy* writes, "Rationalization has been called 'the counterfeit of reason.' It is possible to develop an elaborate reasoning process to steer attention away from one's own deficiencies."[2] When we rationalize, we search for ways to justify our negative actions or feelings. The prospect of having to deal directly with our guilt is painful, so we develop elaborate reasons why we needn't feel the guilt in the first place.

In Jim's case, he not only minimized his guilt feelings, but also rationalized the situation by telling himself, *That's the way it's done in our profession. The ethical guidelines are too restrictive and don't take into account the day-to-day requirements of the business.* In order to live with the unethical practices and his guilt feelings, he had to rationalize and justify his actions.

Through rationalization, we allow ourselves to engage in undesirable behaviors. While on a diet, we may tell ourselves that the chocolate cake is just a boost to our morale. If we neglect to fulfill our responsibility to someone, we may tell ourselves that the person doesn't always fulfill *his* responsibility; therefore it's okay if we don't. When we don't help someone in need, we may tell ourselves that someone else will come along who is better qualified to help. We do these and similar things to justify our behavior and to smooth over our guilt feelings.

Psychoanalysts estimate that we use 50 to 60 percent of our mental energy keeping unwanted wishes and emotions locked inside. They believe *repression* is one of our preferred weapons in the war against painful thoughts and feelings.

Repression and *denial* are our unconscious ways of becoming blinded to negative feelings. We construct a fantasy world in which guilt is not allowed. We put on blinders and pretend that our guilt feelings don't exist, that they are just a figment of our imagination.

Denying guilt's existence can have negative repercussions. Good guilt serves as a corrective device, helping us to sense our wrongdoing and correct it. When we turn off this behavior-correcting mechanism, we repeat the same mistakes over and over again. Rather than openly acknowledging our errors and feeling remorse, we ignore the situation altogether. As you can imagine, repression and denial are hard to detect and destructive to our personal and spiritual growth. Becoming more aware of guilt's presence will help us detect our tendencies to repress it.

Spiritual Masks

The ways we inappropriately deal with guilt in the spiritual realm overlap with several of the other areas mentioned above. When overcome with guilt we may condemn ourselves and incorrectly assume that God is also condemning us. We may deny ourselves pleasure or possessions as a means of atonement. We may seek to cleanse ourselves from our sins through a frenzy of Christian service. Or we may begin to avoid God or turn from our faith because of the burden of our guilt. All of these attempts at running from guilt serve only to alienate us from the One who is able to heal and help us.

When destructive guilt claims our hearts and minds, we forget about God's forgiveness, mercy and grace and focus on his wrath, justice and judgment. Our perspective becomes narrow and negative and our understanding of God's love becomes distorted and discouraging. The numerous ways we effectively and ineffectively deal with the spiritual nature of guilt will be explored at more length in later chapters.

Recognizing, Removing and Replacing the Masks

"We wear masks, and with practice we do it better and better, and they serve us well—except that it gets very lonely inside the mask because inside the mask . . . is a person who both longs to be known and fears to be known."³ Which masks do *you* use? What guilt cover-ups do you employ most? What keeps you from looking at guilt face to face? Each of us generally uses only a few of these guilt cover-ups, though we may draw upon many of them from time to time. We find those masks that seem to fit the best and use them again and again.

   If we are to win the battle, we need to

☐ *recognize* the unhealthy masks we use to deal with guilt. As you read through the chapter, try to identify those masks you tend to use.

☐ *remove* these destructive masks so that we can face guilt squarely. When you discover (uncover) a mask, ask yourself why you are using the mask and why you are feeling guilty. Once you remove the masks you can face guilt directly. It's hard to box an elusive opponent.

☐ *replace* them with new, healthier means of dealing with guilt. Future chapters explore how to deal with both good and bad guilt.

   It is only as we take these steps that we will break free of the masks we have created for ourselves.

Application Questions

   1. Did you identify with any of the people in this chapter?
   2. How do masks trap guilt inside you?
   3. We use many of the masks at one time or another but use several of the masks most of the time. What masks do you use most?

Prayer

Lord, please help us uncover the masks we use in our attempts to deal with guilt. You are able to help us overcome our ineffective ways of facing guilt. Thank you. Amen.

TEN

Guilt-Driven Disguises

*J*ames came to counseling seeking help for "the mess I've made of my relationships." He explained that he was uncomfortable around others and described how he had immersed himself in a particular hobby. "My wife is fed up with me because she says I should spend more time with the family. And whenever she suggests going out or inviting people over, I refuse. She says I'm too wrapped up in my hobby. She said that if I don't do something about it, she will."

As time progressed, James opened up and shared deep feelings of inadequacy as a husband and father. His guilt led him to avoid his family as well as any possible public humiliation, so he avoided people altogether. He felt his family would be better off if he wasn't around. He had become reclusive, occupying his time with his hobby. Slowly James began to realize that his avoidance of people and his obsession with his hobby were actually his way of playing hide-and-seek with guilt. He'd hide and hope that guilt wouldn't find him. His avoidance, which began as a temporary mask, had become a permanent disguise.

Many of us find that masks inadequately protect us from guilt, so we develop more pervasive cover-ups. When Adam and Eve experienced the guilt of their sin, they hid from God and covered them-selves. This is our perpetual human tendency—to hide and cover up as a result of our guilt. While masks provide only partial covering, disguises provide a more complete camouflage for who we are and what we are feeling.

With a disguise, we take on an all-encompassing, not easily change-able image, personality or lifestyle. We exchange who we are for some-one or something else who we think will be better able to deal with our unwanted feelings. Our cover-ups become so pervasive that our new identities are sometimes indistinguishable from our real selves. However, as François de La Rochefoucauld wrote, an unfortunate outcome is that "we are so accustomed to disguising ourselves to others, that in the end we become disguised to ourselves."

Guilty States and Traits—Masks and Disguises

Most of the masks mentioned in the last chapter, if used long enough, can easily become ingrained aspects of our personality and who we are. If guilt leads us to self-pity, we can succumb to a life of self-condemnation. Self-destructive behavior can become normal for us, and our tendency to withdraw from or avoid people can become a permanent mode of interacting with others.

Researchers who study guilt have acknowledged the complexity of assessing it. Not only must they differentiate between guilt and guilt feelings (which may or may not be related), but they must also dis-tinguish between what is referred to as "state guilt" and "trait guilt." *State guilt* is our guilty situation or condition. It is transient and temporary. When we have committed a sin, we are in a guilty state. *Trait guilt,* on the other hand, is guilt that has become a fixture in our personality. Feeling guilty is such a part of life that it becomes a characteristic or personality trait. Guilt has enveloped us to the degree that it becomes part of who we are.

It is much the same with masks and disguises. Masks are what we put on to temporarily dissuade the unwanted guilt feelings. Disguises are a more permanent means of dealing with guilt's constant presence.

Many factors contribute to why we act the ways we do. While some of our behaviors are a direct result of guilt, other behaviors are indi-rectly related to it. Whatever the cause, however, guilt is usually involved in one way or another. Although we may wear several different guilt-ridden masks, we generally employ only one guilt-driven disguise. Which of these, if any, do *you* use?

Disguises Based on Work

Darren worked and worked and worked. His insatiable need to prove himself successful set a precedent for his lifestyle and relationships. When choices arose, work would win over family. It was only in his work that Darren felt relief from the guilt he felt for not being the kind of son he thought his dad had wanted. But attempting to appease the guilt from his family of origin, Darren only created fresh guilt for neglecting his own family. This cycle of guilt and work, work and guilt drove Darren to become a *workaholic*—the only way he knew how to avoid his unwanted feelings.

Workaholics work harder and longer in hopes that guilt will go away. As work-minded individuals, we hide in our work, deriving much of our identity from what we do rather than from our character or who we are. "Work, work, work" is our motto. The busier we are, the more numb we become to guilt.

Cherie's time is spent helping with anything and everything at the church and at the Christian school her children attend. While her work is needed and appreciated, it actually serves to cover up her feelings of guilt for not being a better Christian. Cherie's "do-aholic" behavior seems to imply that she believes that faith is not enough to assure her salvation and good standing before God, but that works (good deeds done) are essential as well. If asked, Cherie would deny the belief that salvation comes from works. Her life, however, seems to contradict her theology.

Like the workaholic, the do-aholic's approach to dealing with guilt is to try to alleviate it by works. The work's primary purpose is to lessen the internal pain caused by guilt for actions done or not done in the past, present and future. The do-aholic's service could be club, children or church related. The work done may be benevolent but is actually meant to cover guilt feelings.

Some of us become *obsessive-compulsive,* desperately trying to find a way to get rid of the negative feelings and thoughts associated with guilt. We become obsessive when we have persistent ideas, thoughts or impuses that disturb our daily functioning. Compulsions are behaviors we enact in our attempt to rid ourselves of the obsessive thoughts. These compulsive behaviors are our feeble attempts to deal with unwanted obsessions. If we convince ourselves that a certain behavior will eliminate or appease our shame, then we will do the action over and over and over again, even if it seems ridiculous.

Gina became obsessive about the need for her house to be clean. She scrubbed the bathrooms and dusted daily, and she mopped the kitchen floor and vacuumed twice a day. Her obsessive-compulsive behavior reflected her inner sense of filthiness for her perceived and actual sins. Cleaning the house represented her efforts to cleanse herself of her guilt and sin.

Karyl, a *perfectionist,* was never satisfied with anything she did. Everything had to be perfect, or else she would condemn herself mercilessly. Her drive for personal perfection was fueled by feelings of guilt for not being as good a wife or mother as she thought she should be. She believed that the guilt would subside if she were as perfect as is possible—thus the continual pursuit of an unattainable ideal.

"Try harder" is the motto of perfectionists. We believe we can eliminate guilt if we are as good and as perfect as we can be. Our imperfections scream in our hearts and minds, while our actions continue to strive for perfection. Though we know that perfection is elusive and unattainable, we still try to quell the raging storm within by chasing after this pot of gold. Like the workaholic and the do-aholic, we try to rid ourselves of guilt by works.

Robert achieved many of his personal and professional goals. He graduated first in his class at the university, was elected president of his professional organization and received numerous awards. Due to his feelings of inadequacy and guilt, he had become an *overachiever.* He hoped that with each accomplishment he would feel more adequate and less guilt-driven.

This disguise is commonly worn by those of us who believe that achievements cancel out guilt—the more we achieve, the more guilt we evict and the more worthy we feel. We may also believe that our positive achievements (like the do-aholics' good deeds) atone for our sin. Once again, we fall into the trap of believing that works, achievements and deeds done can rid us of our unwanted emotions.

Action Steps

What can you do to let go of these disguises? To put it simply, stop trying to outwork and outmaneuver guilt.

☐ Accept God's sovereignty, love and forgiveness.

☐ Ask yourself whether your work, service, behavior and achievements are for God's glory or for your guilt.

☐ Admit that your works-oriented life is irreverent and unhealthy.

☐ Address the sources and reasons for your guilt-driven behavior. (Continue reading this book.)

☐ Abstain from trying to erase guilt, earn salvation or atone for sin through your works, service, behavior or achievements.

☐ Ask God to help you change.

☐ Memorize Ephesians 2:8-9: "For it is by grace you have been saved, through faith—and this not from yourselves, it is the gift of God—not by works, so that no one can boast," and Romans 5:8: "But God demonstrates his own love for us in this: While we were still sinners, Christ died for us."

Disguises Based on Personality and Lifestyle

Those of us who are *controllers* attempt to control everything and everyone around us. If we can control our environment, perhaps we can tame the seemingly uncontrollable negative emotions stirring within. Our need to control demonstrates our inability to face the unknown and our insecurities. We see guilt as a reckless car without a driver. We jump in the driver's seat in hopes of gaining control of the wheel and the destination. Like most disguises, however, this only puts us on a collision course.

The *passive-aggressive* person seems compliant on the outside but is usually filled with intense anger (and guilt) on the inside. Sonya felt guilty around her parents. She felt that she never quite lived up to their expectations. When it came time to visit them, she would be sick and unable to go. When she was supposed to call them at an aunt's house, she would lose the phone number. When she was expected to meet them somewhere, her car would break down or run out of gas.

Many of us feel uncomfortable with anger because we consider it an inappropriate emotion. It usually seeps through, however, and manifests itself indirectly in various behaviors. Rather than unveil our negative feelings, we reveal them in subtle and "safe" ways. Rather than face guilt head-on, we allow it to stew until it becomes anger. This anger is then vented in numerous ways against those around us. When we become passive-aggressive, as with most masks and disguises, we often end up heaping more guilt upon ourselves.

Another guilt-escape we use is becoming *dependent* on others. Many of us, overcome with our imperfections, want to turn over the reins of our lives. We don't trust ourselves because we know our sinfulness and guilt. We terminate the rights to govern our life and search for those who will take over and do a better job. We want others to dominate our decision-making because we feel unable to make the right choices. Past decisions have only ended in failure. Dependency lessens our sense of guilt by lessening our sense of responsibility for who we are and what we do. We abdicate all rights and gladly give them to another in hope that this will eliminate guilt's pointing finger.

When guilt speaks words of reproach, we may put on the cloak of self-sacrifice and *self-denial*. To allow ourselves pleasure would only add to our already enormous sense of guilt. So we abstain from anything that may bring positive rewards, because we feel totally undeserving. Our disgrace disallows joy.

An ascetic lifestyle may falsely lead us to believe we can overcome sin and guilt. We sacrifice the "good life" and deny ourselves pleasure as a way to reduce the temptations we face, a way to make amends or a means of self-punishment. Many of us send ourselves into exile, viewing self-denial as payment for guilt.

When our human failings and their accompanying feelings of guilt grow to shameful proportions, we may seclude ourselves from the world and become *separatists*. This seclusion serves either to help us escape public shame and embarrassment or to provide us with a type of punishment, our own private jail sentence. To go into the world would expose our depravity. This guilt disguise restrains our movements, actions and interactions. While some who choose this monastic type of lifestyle do so in order to focus on God, others do so to hide from the raging emotions within, out of fear of public ridicule or desire to punish themselves through self-denial.

If the *avoider* disguise is worn, we spend our energies avoiding all thoughts and actions that may remind us of our guilt. We avoid all contact or mention of people, places and things that are associated with or that trigger any sense of our guilt. Many avoiders are avid sports fans, hobbyists, club members and exercisers. Their unwritten motto is "The busier I am doing other things, the less my mind will dwell on my feelings of guilt." When we choose this disguise, we often spend more time and energy avoiding guilt than it would take to work through it.

Leslie never said no, because she feared displeasing people. Whenever she was asked to do something, whether for church, the women's circle, the missions committee, her children's school or her boss, she would answer in the affirmative. She wanted to please others regardless of any personal sacrifice involved. Somehow she believed that if she were to say no, the guilt would overpower her and leave her disabled for life.

Those of us wearing the *pleaser* disguise hope that niceness will cover up our guilt. If we do as others wish, please others at all costs, don't make waves and are submissive, obedient and kind, perhaps guilt will be obscured from view.

Those who *rescue* spend their time helping others, meeting needs, offering a listening ear. The focus is on helping others with their problems while avoiding direct confrontation of our own. This strategy appears altruistic and admirable but is another means of avoidance.

Michael is a *critical*, negative person. He sees the thorns, not the rose; the storm, not the rainbow. He searches out and finds the imperfections in others and in life's situations. His pessimistic perspective serves to soothe the sense of his own sinfulness. He believes that he'll feel better if he doesn't feel alone in his misery.

Researchers who study people's preferences when feeling "miserable" discovered that it is not so much that "misery loves company" but that "misery loves miserable company." We'd rather have a companion who is also struggling so that we don't feel alone in our misery.

Those of us who wear this disguise search for the imperfections in life in an effort to justify our own. Finding the flaws in others lessens the pain of living with our own. As we identify the numerous blunders around us, we feel less alone in our wretchedness.

Action Steps
Take a good, hard look at who you are and how you react and respond to life.

☐ Accept God's sovereignty, love and forgiveness.

☐ Ask God to help uncover the unhealthy ways you deal with guilt.

☐ Analyze the sources and reasons for your guilt-driven behavior. (Continue reading this book, and consider seeking professional assistance.)

☐ Ask God to help you change these negative behaviors, patterns and characteristics.

☐ Memorize Galatians 2:20: "I have been crucified with Christ and I no longer live, but Christ lives in me. The life I live in the body, I live by faith in the Son of God, who loved me and gave himself for me," and Romans 5:8: "But God demonstrates his own love for us in this: While we were still sinners, Christ died for us."

Disguises Based on Giving Up or Coping
Many of us use *addictions* to help us cope with deep inner guilt and shame, whether it is to food, gambling, drugs, alcohol or something else. We deaden the pain with various substances. For some this is just another form of self-punishment or self-destructive behavior.

When inner feelings of guilt become overwhelming, some of us give up trying to tame them and decide to live out what we believe about ourselves as sinners and *rebels.* Inside we see ourselves as imperfect, hypocritical and worthless. We know our own sinful hearts and thoughts. The dichotomy between who we are supposed to be as Christians and how we see ourselves is too great and too painful to bear, so we become rebellious. We feel we deserve a sinful life because it is more closely akin to our beliefs about ourselves. We choose the guilt of making "wrong" choices over the endless inner guilt of trying to be good and failing. We simply substitute one guilt for another.

The sexually abused young woman who becomes promiscuous may be giving in to an enormous burden of undeserved guilt. Her sexual rebellion may reflect feelings of hopelessness in response to the devastating guilt and shame she feels as well as reinforcing her negative thoughts about herself.

The *hedonist's* motto is "If you can't beat 'em, join 'em." He chooses to "live it up" and to "eat, drink and be merry" because whether he abstains or engages in sinful behavior, guilt is ever-present. Since he's in a lose-lose proposition, why not enjoy himself? Though this brings momentary pleasure, it serves to dig a deeper hole into which guilt pours its foundation.

Action Steps
Stop trying to deaden the pain. Don't give up or give in. Hang in there and keep on fighting—fight to regain a sense of how precious you are to a God who unconditionally loves you.

☐ Accept God's sovereignty, love and forgiveness.

☐ Acknowledge that your coping mechanisms are destructive.

☐ Address the sources and reasons for your guilt-driven behavior. (Continue reading this book.)

☐ Access a support group (twelve-step, survivors, a Bible study) and professional or pastoral assistance.

☐ Abstain from your unhealthy patterns.

☐ Ask God to help you overcome and change these negative behaviors and coping mechanisms.

☐ Memorize 1 John 4:4: "You, dear children, are from God and have overcome them, because the one who is in you is greater than the one who is in the world"; Ephesians 3:12, 16: "In him and through faith in him we may approach God with freedom and confidence. . . . I pray that . . . he may strengthen you with power through his Spirit in your inner being"; and Romans 5:8: "But God demonstrates his own love for us in this: While we were still sinners, Christ died for us."

Dealing with Guilt
We masquerade in hopes of fooling guilt's watchful eye. We mistakenly think that we can hide from guilt by using these various disguises. "The ways we choose to avoid guilt are far more dangerous than facing guilt itself. Mistakenly, we try to convince ourselves we must at any cost flee the overpowering oppression of guilt rather than learn its causes."[1]

If we are to survive our encounters with guilt, we must be willing to learn its causes. We must also be willing to remove the masks and disguises we use to defend ourselves. These protective layers, meant to keep guilt out, trap guilt inside and obstruct our relationship with God.

Application Questions
1. Which disguises, if any, do you use?
2. Which of these disguises do you recognize among people you know?
3. Can you identify Bible characters who used some of these disguises?
4. Why do you use the disguises? In what ways do you find them helpful? harmful?
5. What would you add to the action steps to make them more helpful?

Prayer
Lord, we praise you that with you on our side, we are able to overcome. Help us to depend completely on you as we strive to remove the disguises that keep us from facing guilt and get in our way of understanding your grace and love. Amen.

E L E V E N

The All-Consuming Battle

*A*s soon as I passed the police car I looked at my speedometer to see how fast I was going. As I slowed down, I noticed that the police car pulled out and was following me. I frantically tried to remember the speed limit for that stretch of road. My mind started racing (hoping that the car hadn't been), thinking about how I would respond to the officer and mustering all of my plausible and possible excuses. When the police car turned off the road, I was relieved and stopped developing my defense.

When Barry forgot an important meeting, he told his boss, "My kids have been sick, my car broke down, and I just found out that our neighbor's niece committed suicide." Justifying an affair, Wanda said that her kids drove her crazy, she didn't like living in the country and her husband was a workaholic. And when Josephine and her two sisters confronted their alcoholic father with allegations of sexual abuse, he said it must have been when he was drunk, because he didn't remember having abused them.

When we are stopped for speeding or confronted about a mistake, when we've missed a deadline, forgotten a promise or committed a sin, one of our instinctual responses is to develop a defense. We make excuses, explain our special exception and present our plea of innocence or, at least, semi-innocence. Rather than accept our error, we make excuses. Rather than admit our blunder, we get ready for battle. Why? Because if we admit wrong, we must face our guilt.

Guilt feelings are often met with a response of "Red alert!" or "Battle stations!" When we feel guilty, our built-in defense mechanisms are triggered into action. Whether accused rightly or wrongly, by ourselves (our conscience) or someone else, we respond with a fight-flight instinct much like that of animals. Like a cat sensing danger, we either flee from the situation or arch our backs, expose our claws, hiss and get ready to fight back. We fight for our rights, our honor, our character, for what we believe in, for justice. More commonly, we fight against guilt rather than a wrong accusation. We view guilt as the enemy and give it much more power, attention, time and energy than it deserves. We often turn our encounters with guilt into an ongoing, all-consuming battle.

We respond to perceived attacks by *fighting, fleeing or surrendering*. When we choose to *flee* from guilt, we elude capture by using the masks and disguises discussed in the last two chapters. We try to camouflage our feelings and conceal our fears. In order to avoid capture, we cover up our true thoughts and feelings. If we choose to *fight*, we gear up for what we assume will be a long, hard battle. If we *surrender*, we give up and turn ourselves over to the opponent.

Let's examine these last two battle plans more closely.

Fight

When we decide to fight guilt, we take on a formidable opponent. We gather all of our resources and carefully plan our defense. We build thick, strong walls and stand ready to defend our territory at all times because we believe that guilt will capture our emotional well-being. We automatically start preparing our defense when either a confrontation or our conscience leaves us feeling guilty. Without first evaluating the opponent's power, size and strength, we begin preparations for an all-out war. We use up too much of our valuable time and energy in this constant state of battle readiness, and our defenses become weary and worn.

It's like preparing for a trial. When someone is accused, lawyers immediately begin to expend an enormous amount of time and energy preparing a defense. Before the trial, they gather facts, information, support, documentation, testimonies and more. Numerous hours are spent in an effort to establish the innocence of the accused—regardless of whether he or she *is* innocent.

If innocence cannot be established, the defense attorneys might seek to distort, distract or explain away the accusations. They look for possible alternative explanations for the accused's behavior—a difficult past, a misunderstanding, "temporary insanity" or other reasons. Witnesses are identified and contacted to serve as positive character references. And the jury is selected carefully, since each side wants people sympathetic to its cause.

The defense becomes suspicious of the prosecution, perhaps labeling them as jealous, vindictive opponents. All potential liabilities and possible enemies in the case are identified, and documentation is gathered to discredit them. The other side's witnesses are questioned mercilessly in an attempt to refute their testimony. Defense lawyers guard their actions, watch what they say and are careful in their associations—they mustn't jeopardize the defense. Relationships may suffer because of a defensive, cautious demeanor, and the attorneys sacrifice valuable time and resources amassing their defense.

Doubt is raised, motive is uncertain, and the process is questioned. Hundreds if not thousands of hours and much money are spent in defense of the one accused of a wrongdoing.

When you and I are accused of a wrongdoing, confronted with a character flaw or faced with our faults, we also begin formulating our defense. We remember all the times we acted contrary to the alleged inappropriate behavior. We think of all the people who will stand by us and defend us—people afraid to tell it like it is, people who fear confrontation or those who agree with us no matter what. We seek to discredit our accusers in hopes of discrediting their accusations. We may even begin to play the role of the martyr and to feel self-righteous. We view our persecution as undeserved. We may begin to spiritualize the experience, proclaiming that we are "suffering for the Lord."

Guilt Depletes Our Resources

Guilt drains emotional, physical and mental energy and consumes valuable time. We focus our time and energy on unjust allegations rather than on accusations that are true. We justify ourselves when we should examine ourselves. We concern ourselves with our rights when we should concern ourselves more with diligent stewardship of our resources.

When Adam and Eve ate the forbidden fruit, sin and guilt entered the world. After their disobedience, life was no longer worry-free. Time and energy were needed to find a place to stay, clothes to wear and food to eat. Today not only do we spend time and resources taking care of our daily needs, we also spend a lot of time and energy hiding and defending ourselves against guilt. Guilt has definitely been depleting our resources since it came on the scene!

Guilt is a time-waster, a resource-user and an energy-drainer. It ravages our relationships, plunders our productivity and crushes our creativity.

Surrender

We have seen that fighting is ineffective and time-consuming. Therefore let's examine our other option—to surrender. When faced with guilt some of us would rather surrender than fight. But immediate, unconditional surrender can be equally damaging and draining when it is prompted by fear of pain or fear of defeat in the battle against guilt. This is not a surrendering to God but a surrendering to guilt's control. Sometimes when we answer, "Yes, I am guilty," we do so only to avoid further exposure, not wanting to face guilt directly. *This admission of guilt is more of a concession than a confession.*

The quick surrender serves to lessen the amount of guilt that is placed before the public eye. Rather than "go to trial," we "settle out of court" as soon as possible. We don't want our sinful thoughts and deeds exposed through questioning on the witness stand.

This unconditional, immediate surrender only strengthens guilt's power over us. We concede without examining whether the guilt is good or bad, true or false. When we surrender we generally take on the role of judge, prosecutor, defense attorney and jury. We decide the verdict and the penalty without listening to any evidence. Rather than proclaim a mistrial, we begin serving our sentence without question. We may end up spending much of our time and energy being needlessly punished.

While surrendering may seem time-efficient, it is not. Those who surrender decide that their wretched soul deserves harsh punishment, which they will self-inflict. Like fighting, self-punishment is time-consuming. Tournier writes,

> Numerous illnesses, both physical and nervous, and even accidents, or frustrations in social or professional life are revealed by psychoanalysis to be attempts at the expiation of guilt which is wholly unconscious. It is a form of punishment which the sufferer administers to himself, and it goes on repeating itself indefinitely with a kind of inexorable fatality.[1]

We spend time and energy dealing with our disorders and avoiding our issues—many of them developed directly or indirectly because of our need to "pay" for our sinfulness. Harlan Wechsler explains, "People get sick and fail to seek medical help, for they see their illnesses as a punishment they deserve. Others develop eating disorders, sleeping disorders, and personality disorders galore in order to punish themselves in secret ways for the unsavory deeds they have committed."[2]

Unconditional surrender brings self-punishment that robs us of valuable time. Guilt has gained another victory, distracting us from the real issues behind the guilt and from a loving, forgiving God.

Abandoning Our Battle Plans

It is apparent that our means of dealing with guilt have proven ineffective. The damage is extensive, our resources are depleted, and our morale is discouragingly low. We are facing defeat and must abandon our unsuccessful plans.

Battle Plans Against Guilt

Strategies	Flee	Fight	Surrender
Tactics	Hide, using masks and disguises	Defend ourselves	Give up and begin self-punishment

How do we break out of this doomed situation? We must start by identifying the many masks and disguises we wear in our attempts to *flee* from guilt. As we have seen, time and energy are snatched from us as we develop and maintain these cover-ups. We must also admit our tendency to expend far too much of our time and energy *fighting* guilt. We must lower our defenses, put down our weapons and call for a cease-fire. Let's take a good, long, hard look at the enemy *before* developing our battle plan and *before* calling out the troops. And we must not *surrender* prematurely. We mustn't admit defeat before examining our motives. To serve a sentence for false guilt and to initiate self-punishment is not only time-consuming but, more important, emotionally harmful.

We must regain a sense of priorities. *Our time should not be spent defending against guilt but depending on God.* He, not guilt, should be the focus of our energies.

Application Questions

1. Do you spend a lot of time and energy defending yourself when accused of a wrongdoing? What would be a more effective course of action?

2. Do you sometimes "surrender" prematurely to guilt to avoid both scrutiny and facing the root of the problem? What are you afraid of?

3. Reread the quotes by Tournier and Wechsler. If you find yourself engaging in any self-punitive behavior, what do you hope to gain from it?

4. What can you do to change your strategy in dealing with guilt, whether good or bad guilt?

Prayer

Lord, help us to depend on you rather than defend ourselves against guilt. We desire to surrender our lives to you and not to guilt. Amen.

TWELVE

A Winning Strategy

*W*e live near the trailhead of a nature preserve in the mountains. A few feet beyond the entrance is a display informing hikers, bird-watchers and nature-lovers about the types of trees, flowers and wild-life in the area. A warning is posted about mountain lions, telling hikers what they should do if they encounter one.

A recent headline in our local paper told of a man who came upon a mountain lion while jogging with his dog. The startled beast began chasing the man with great speed and determination. Fortunately the man remembered the instructions. He stopped, turned around and faced the mountain lion. Surprised, it ceased its chase and walked away.

We human beings are not naturally inclined to turn and face some-thing that we find frightening. Our tendency is not to look the enemy in the eye but to keep on running.

I have found in my own life and in the lives of those I counsel that when we face the things we dread, we usually find them to be less powerful in reality than we had imagined them to be. What appears to be an enormous monster's shadow is actually that of a tiny mouse standing in front of a light. The more we view something with fear and trepidation, the bigger and more powerful it gets. All too often we spend more energy avoiding our fears than dealing with them. When we face our fears, we discover how much we distorted their significance and power.

Guilt is like the mountain lion. We must turn and face it.

Many in our culture espouse the belief that we should strive to be guilt-free. Guilt is to be abolished, nullified and excommunicated. We are encouraged to ignore guilt, to pretend it doesn't exist. Whereas society says we should be guilt-free, God says that we should be guilt-filled. As we begin to see our guilt from his perspective we should be more acutely aware of our desperate need for him.

God's Paradoxical Battle Plan

The Bible is full of paradoxical situations or analogies. We are told in Matthew 10:39 that "whoever finds his life will lose it, and whoever loses his life for my sake will find it." Mark 10:31 informs us, "But many who are first will be last, and the last first." And again we read, " 'No one can see the kingdom of God unless he is born again.' 'How can a man be born when he is old?' Nicodemus asked" (Jn 3:3-4).

Dealing with guilt presents us with another paradox: in order to rid ourselves of guilt we must take hold of our guilty nature. In order to let go of excess guilt we must embrace our guilt-stained selves.

Perhaps you have heard of the monkey trying to get some candy out of a jar. He puts his hand in and grabs the treat but finds that he cannot remove his hand from the jar and hang on to the candy at the same time. The harder he tries, the more frustrated he becomes. The monkey cannot free his hand from the jar until he is willing to give up what he is clinging to so fiercely. If he refuses to let go, he will be forced to adjust to life without full use of both hands.

Like the monkey, we cling to our feeble attempts to alleviate guilt. We don't want to let go of our masks, our disguises, our defenses or our spiritual attempts to atone for our guilt. But when we do let go of these ineffective strategies, we are freed from the burden of always striving against and struggling with guilt. This freedom enables us to better serve God as we come to him with both a contrite heart and two hands!

Another paradox exists in our battle with guilt. In order to end the struggle and win the fight, we must surrender—not the quick surrender of those avoiding exposure and desiring self-sentencing, but unconditional surrender to God's plan. Whereas our tendency is to fight or flee, to set up defenses or elude guilt, God wants us to surrender to him. God's way to victory is through surrender of our wills to his ways. To win the battle we must begin waving the white flag, not to guilt, but to God.

To decrease our guilt, we must first increase our awareness of our guilty state. By embracing our guilt and admitting our fallen nature, we increase our need for God and decrease the power of excessive, unnecessary guilt.

When we embrace guilt, we acknowledge our sinful nature and the ease with which we can succumb to temptations. We accept our human weaknesses and our selfish, sinful inclinations. We must acknowledge, "*I AM A SINNER* and as such, have the capacity to send Jews to the gas chambers, rape, murder, adultery, etc. *This* must be embraced, that *even I* could do this. To own yourself in this way, by God's grace, is a buffer against sin. We do not embrace the 'sinful self' but the self which is sinful."[1]

God's strategy is to face and embrace guilt. As we embrace guilt we are freed from our obsession with it. It no longer possesses us. We no longer need to justify ourselves, because we are willing to admit our imperfections and our guilt. We no longer need to dodge it, because we've come to peace with the fact that it is unavoidable and even helpful.

Guilt is helpful when it forces us to the cross. The totality of our guilt should make us realize the totality of our need for God. We surrender and admit that Jesus is all-sufficient. We cannot earn his favor or merit his love. It is a wondrous gift, undeserved and free. Our profound sense of guilt brings an awareness of the depth of his amazing grace.

The many ways we attempt to deal with guilt demonstrate our foolish belief that we should somehow be able to rid ourselves of it through our own efforts. We can't. The fact that nothing we can do can rid ourselves of guilt should in and of itself be freeing. Only God can declare us wretches worthy of love and service (Jn 3:16; Rom 5:8;

1 Tim 1:12), and only he can offer the forgiveness we need. The key to the guilt dilemma is to accept rather than disown our guilt, to embrace rather than elude it. As we face our guilt, we are freed from its negative grasp, free to take hold of our Redeemer—with two hands.

The Extent of Guilt

In Leviticus, the "Book of the Law," we are told that those who sin "unintentionally" or "unknowingly" are still guilty. Leviticus told the Israelites how to deal with sin and guilt. When the whole community (4:13), a leader (4:22) or a member of the community (4:27) "sins unintentionally and does what is forbidden in any of the LORD's commands, even though [they are] unaware of the matter, they are guilty" (4:13). God's Word convicts us of guilt even when we have erred unaware. Not only sinful thoughts, words and deeds that we knowingly commit but also those that we do unknowingly are contrary to God's ways.

The psalmist laments, "You know my folly, O God; my guilt is not hidden from you. . . . You have set our iniquities before you, our secret sins in the light of your presence" (Ps 69:5; 90:8). Both the known and unknown, the acknowledged and secret, the willful and hidden sins we commit are exposed in God's presence. We stand clothed in our sinfulness before him. There is no escape.

"If you, O LORD, kept a record of sins, O Lord, who could stand?" (Ps 130:3). Psalm 143:2 declares, "No one living is righteous before you." No one can stand and no one is righteous before God. We can easily echo the psalmist's lament, "My guilt has overwhelmed me like a burden too heavy to bear" (Ps 38:4).

Lest we think that the God of the New Testament changed his perspective on the totality of our guilt, let's take another look. Under the law, a person was guilty of sin if he committed such acts as adultery, theft and murder. Judging the matter was quite clear-cut: you either did or didn't sin. But Jesus radically changed the ground rules when he told the multitudes in the Sermon on the Mount that not only is adultery considered a sin, so is lusting after someone; not only is stealing wrong, so are envy, jealousy and coveting; not only is murder a sin, so is harboring anger.

Tournier writes,

The drift of the Sermon on the Mount is not that of a recipe for freedom from guilt by meritorious conduct. Just the opposite—it is the shattering word which convicts of murder a man who has done no killing, of adultery the man who has not committed the act, of perjury one who is not foresworn, of hatred one who boasted of his love, of hypocrisy the man who was noted for his piety. . . . A man who seeks to cleanse himself of guilt becomes even more heavily burdened with it.[2]

Jesus' strategy for dealing with guilt is to admit its inescapable nature, to acknowledge its pervasiveness. Tournier points out that the Sermon on the Mount increased rather than decreased our guilt by declaring not only our actions and deeds guilty but also our thoughts, motives and intentions. With the new ground rules, the many dos and don'ts of the Sermon on the Mount reinforce the all-encompassing, inescapable nature of our guilt. No matter how hard we try, we will inevitably, undeniably fail.

James 2:10 affirms this thought: "For whoever keeps the whole law and yet stumbles at just one point is guilty of breaking all of it." How can we not occasionally stumble? How are we to be holy and pure in all things at all times? The task is not just overwhelming—it is impossible.

Romans 3:23 clarifies the matter for us: "*All* have sinned and fall short of the glory of God." Not one of us can evade the fact that we sin, we fall short, we stumble. Like those accusing the woman of adultery, who of us is left to condemn her? " 'If any one of you is without sin, let him be the first to throw a stone at her.' . . . At this, those who heard began to go away one at a time" (Jn 8:7, 9). None of us is without sin, none of us is guilt-free.

We always have hidden faults, unintentional acts, unconscious attitudes or wrongful thoughts. Our perpetually guilty state leaves no room for doubt, no chance for reprieve. *We have a sinful nature that cannot be erased, changed or reversed.*

When we first realize there is nothing we can do to hide from guilt, our soul is filled either with terror or with peace. Sooner or later we must admit guilt's prevalence and permanence in our lives. We must come face to face with the unwanted fact that our sin and guilt are inevitable, inescapable and universal.

How do we respond when we can't ignore or pretend that guilt doesn't exist? What do we do once we know that no matter what we do, we remain guilty? "The central question of the Bible and of all religion is, 'How can human beings be blameless before God?' In other words, how can we get free of the crushing sense of guilt and insecurity that dogs our every step? How can we have peace?"[3]

The Verdict: Guilty—But Not Condemned

Let's return to the courtroom illustration. The accused stands before the judge. Rather than beginning a strategic defense aimed at self-exoneration and accuser defamation, the individual confesses, "Yes, I am guilty. I am imperfect. I made a mistake. I am sorry. What must I do to make amends?"

This confession is based on pure and simple fact. It is not made in order to receive a lighter sentence, avoid pain or flee from fears; it is made from a contrite heart. It is a clear acknowledgment of the truth. Rather than spend tremendous effort justifying our actions, we should face our guilt and respond like the defendant: "Yes, I am guilty."

We are guilty. Why try to run, cover, hide, pretend, project or deny it? Why try to fight, flee or surrender? Why become legalistic, self-denying or works-oriented? Our feeble yet arduous attempts to lessen our guilt in order to gain God's favor or earn his forgiveness are ludicrous. Guilt is a fact of our human condition before God. Until we accept this fact, we will be plagued by guilt's crushing weight and haunted by its overriding presence.

God's strategy for dealing with guilt first requires that we accept the totality of our guilt and acknowledge that we cannot overcome it in and of ourselves. When we acknowledge our guilt-ridden nature, we no longer need to fear the trial, the prosecution or the sentencing, because we have admitted our guilt, received God's forgiveness and moved on. While others are still amassing defensive strategies or busy putting on masks and disguises, we are free to concern ourselves more with the Lord's will than our ways.

As we come to accept our thorough sinfulness, we find comfort in the rest of the story of the woman caught in adultery. Jesus asked her, "Has no one condemned you?" "No one, sir," she said. The accusers had gone, unable to condemn her, because none of them were without sin. Only Jesus remained. He could have condemned her because he was without sin. And yet he told her, just as he tells us today, "Then neither do I condemn you" (Jn 8:9-11).

The True Enemy

In order to gain ground against guilt it may be helpful to view it as an ally rather than an alien foe. Why? Because guilt guides us to God. As we embrace our supposed enemy, it becomes our comrade and shows us the way to safety. When we view guilt as the enemy, we respond with defensiveness. When we view guilt as a friend, we respond with dependence on God.

If guilt is not the enemy, then who or what is? Perhaps the true enemy is our attempt at self-atonement or our propensity toward self-justification rather than justification by faith. Perhaps it is the masks and disguises we use which actually trap guilt inside. Perhaps it is our tendency to try to earn God's favor and forgiveness by rigidly following certain rules and regulations, doing good deeds or acting pious and penitent.

Is guilt the enemy? No. The enemy is our response to guilt. As we identify our true adversary, we are better able to fight the battle.

Our Response	God's Plan
Fight, flee or surrender	Surrender to God's perspective on guilt
Avoid or annihilate guilt	Embrace guilt
Get rid of guilt	Get rid of our ineffective ways of dealing with guilt
Run from guilt	Face guilt
Become less burdened by guilt	Increase our sense of guilt before God
Deny guilt's pervasiveness	Acknowledge the inescapable nature of our guilt
Decrease awareness of guilt	Increase awareness of guilty nature
Be guilt-free	Be guilt-filled—to realize our need for God
Guilt is the enemy	Guilt is a comrade
Rely on our "goodness"	Rely on God's grace
Solutions: use masks, disguises, elaborate defenses, religiosity	Solution: atonement in Christ Jesus

At the Battle of Bunker Hill on June 17, 1775, William Prescott instructed the troops, "Don't fire until you see the whites of their eyes." When we take off our masks and disguises and set aside our elaborate defenses, we are finally able to see guilt close enough to see "the whites of its eyes." Before, we were so busy protecting ourselves that we never turned to face it. With this new perspective, we can begin the process of distinguishing the foe from the friend, good guilt from bad guilt.

Application Questions
1. Who do you think is the true enemy? Bad guilt? Our ineffective responses?
2. What keeps you from turning to face guilt?
3. Is guilt our friend or our foe?

Prayer
Lord, we desire to follow your plan for dealing with guilt. Help us to face it rather than run and hide from it. We want to rely on your grace rather than our "goodness," and we admit our guilty nature. We thank you for providing atonement in Christ Jesus. Amen.

THIRTEEN

Identifying the Enemy

After I spoke to a church group about guilt, a medical doctor told me his story. His oldest sister came to his hospital for a surgery that was dangerous yet successful. During the recovery, however, she developed a staph infection, and she died a week later. Though the doctor was not the attending physician and the hospital had not been negligent, he still felt responsible. The doctor told me that he felt confused and angry for quite a while before he realized that what he was really feeling was guilt. Once he identified the root of what he was feeling, he was better able to deal with it.

In battle, it is imperative that soldiers know how to identify the enemy. If not, they might injure innocent people or one of their comrades. In World War II, for example, the Allied forces knew who the enemy was. Their mission was to stop Hitler's army. The soldiers knew how to identify the enemy's uniform, insignia and gear. The success of the war effort depended on their ability to recognize the foe.

Our task with guilt is much the same. Like the doctor, we do not always clearly know that it is guilt that plagues us. The outcome of our battle against bad guilt depends on our ability to identify it. We know our enemy—not all guilt, but only that which is illegitimate, and our faulty means of dealing with it. We have two tactics: to discontinue our ineffective ways of dealing with guilt and to minimize the amount of false guilt we experience.

Previous chapters helped us with our first task—recognizing our many unhelpful means of dealing with guilt. We discovered that our inappropriate strategies hinder us more than help us. By exposing our feeble and ineffective maneuvers we increase our chances for spiritual victory. We learned of our need to embrace rather than evade guilt, using it to prod us on to spiritual growth and maturity.

Our next task, then, is to diminish bad guilt's role in our lives. In order to do this, we must improve our skills at recognizing it. This is a challenging job, because bad guilt generally works undercover. It doesn't wear a uniform, sport an emblem or speak in a foreign tongue. It's hard to fight an enemy that is well camouflaged. At times it seems we are shadow-boxing an invisible opponent.

Distinguishing Between Good Guilt and Bad Guilt

How can we improve our ability to differentiate between good and bad guilt? *Bad* guilt distracts us from focusing on God's will. It seduces us into excessive and obsessive behaviors and thoughts, draining our energy and depleting our spiritual life. This is the guilt that must be abolished. *Good* guilt is the friend that leads us to our loving God, in whom we find freedom and forgiveness. This is the guilt we should experience when we don't obey God, turning away from his will, commands and desires. It forces us to reexamine where we're headed.

On distinguishing between good and bad guilt, one survey respondent commented, "Good guilt says, 'I have a problem. I am a sinner. I need help—I need God.' Bad guilt says, 'I am a problem. I am a sinner. I am a terrible person. I am worthless. I can never change.' " *Good guilt is meant to trigger good change.*

The table below shows some of the distinctions between good and bad guilt.

Good Guilt	Bad Guilt
occurs when we don't obey God—his will, plan, commands and desires	occurs when we attempt to obey people—the ways of the world
is personal, internal	is superficial, external
has unchangeable standards	has changeable standards
is determined by God	is determined by society, expectations, culture
is led by the Holy Spirit	is led by the world
convicts	condemns
involves remorse and repentance	involves regrets and repetition
offers forgiveness	offers shame
offers grace	offers judgment
is releasing	is restrictive
is time-giving	is time-consuming
gives joy and inner peace	gives anger and fear
result: a contrite heart	result: a defensive or hiding heart

When asked, "When shouldn't you feel guilty?" one young woman responded, "We shouldn't feel guilty when we haven't done anything wrong or sinful." She then said, "I wish I could heed my own advice."

When Does Bad Guilt Occur?

Bad guilt occurs when we are listening to the *wrong judge* or following the *wrong law*. We will easily become victims of false guilt when we allow society, family, friends and others to judge us and determine the standards by which we should live. God is our righteous judge. When we try to fulfill the wrong law or please the wrong judge, we will inevitably experience excess guilt.

One person wrote that bad guilt is "guilt that leads us away from salvation." Any guilt that is unnecessary or excessive is unhealthy.

Bad guilt occurs when . . .

☐ we feel guilty when we aren't guilty:
  our self-expectations are unrealistic or inapplicable
  we take on the guilt that another places on us (falsely imposed guilt)
  we cling to regrets
  we follow others' excessive laws or allow others, rather than God, to be our judge

☐ we feel excessive guilt:
  we take on more guilt than our offense deserves (we punish ourselves disproportionately to our offense)
  our list of "sinful" behaviors is too extensive and legalistic

☐ we continue to feel guilty after God has forgiven us:
  we don't fully appropriate God's forgiveness
  we don't forgive ourselves

When Should Good Guilt Occur?

From the Bible we know what is and isn't sinful. Though every specific deed is not addressed, it gives us guidelines to help us determine what is pleasing to God and what is not. First, Scripture instructs us not to engage in certain behaviors or thoughts (adultery, murder, theft, grumbling, gossip, slander and so forth). Second, we are told that we should refrain from actions that might cause another to stumble (actions that in and of themselves are not necessarily sinful). Third, we should not perpetuate behaviors or thoughts that are unhealthy or destructive (habits, obsessions). Fourth, we should follow God's will for us individually. That is, if we are called to go to Nineveh, we are disobeying God if we get in a boat going the opposite direction. Last, we should obey most of the governmental laws, rules and regulations under which we live. Beyond these criteria, we find much freedom from guilt—*if* we can keep from falling into the guilt traps set along life's road.

Sin occurs when . . .

☐ we violate God's laws

☐ we cause another to stumble

☐ our behaviors or thoughts become unhealthy and destructive (habits, obsessions)

☐ we disobey God's will, plan or desire for each of us individually

☐ we disobey the laws of the society in which we live (though there are some exceptions)

As we draw nearer to God, fellowship with others, worship, participate in Bible study and pray, we develop a heart that desires to know him and his ways. The more we know him, the more we learn what is and isn't sin. This helps in our quest to distinguish between good and bad guilt. When we commit a sin we should feel good guilt. When we do something that is not sinful and yet feel guilty, we can usually assume that it is bad guilt.

Questions That Can Help

We must test, check and evaluate our guilt feelings before we accept them as accurate, reliable indicators of guilt. Although guilt feelings may alert us to some sin or perceived sin, as we've discussed previously, we mustn't accept them at face value until they've been cross-examined. Harlan Wechsler agrees: "You shouldn't feel guilty when there is insufficient reason for you to feel that way. Cross-examine the guilt. Let it check out the facts."[1] Our task, then, is to develop helpful interrogation skills.

When we find ourselves feeling guilty and are unsure of the source—is it from Satan, self, society or God?—we must ask these questions:

1. Why am I feeling guilty? What did (didn't) I do? (Am I responsible?)

2. Is what I did wrong or sinful according to God's Word (or against the law)?

3. Is what I did wrong or sinful according to God's plan or will for *me?*

4. Is there something I must confess, for which I must ask forgiveness and make amends?

As we ask the first question, we examine the underlying cause of our guilt. We also stop to ask ourselves if we were responsible. The person who has been abused may feel guilty but is not responsible for the abuse. The person who steals, however, is both guilty and responsible for the theft.

The second question forces us to look to God's Word (and our legal system) to see if we have actually committed a transgression. The more familiar we are with God's Word, the better we will know if our words, thoughts or deeds are sinful.

In order to answer the third question regarding God's personal plan for each of us, we may need to seek those who are spiritually mature for confirmation. Proverbs advises us, "For lack of guidance a nation falls, but many advisers make victory sure. . . . A wise man listens to advice" (11:14; 12:15). Since we do not always clearly know what God's will is for us, it may be wise, when in doubt, to ask someone we know and trust for guidance, input and advice. Often we are so emotionally involved that we are unable to see the forest for the trees.

The last question is a call to action if we answered either questions 2 or 3 in the affirmative. If I have indeed sinned according to society's laws, God's Word or God's will for me, then I must confess and make amends.

These questions serve as helpful guidelines to assist in the process of distinguishing good from bad guilt. Not all responses are clear-cut and obvious, however. The answers to the questions may need to address not only the specific act that was or wasn't done but also the circumstances, our attitude and thoughts, our past experiences and any other people involved. Two different people doing the same thing might have opposite responses. One person's guilt feelings may be good guilt, the result of an actual sin. For another person the guilt feelings for the same action may be based on false guilt and need to be shed.

If I'm feeling guilty, I ask myself the first question: *Why am I feeling guilty? What did or didn't I do?* I might answer: *I feel guilty for not writing a letter to a particular friend.* As I ask myself question 2, I discover that nowhere in God's Word does it say that it is a sin not to write a letter. Therefore I answer question 2 with a no. Likewise I might answer question 3 with a no, because I am not disobeying God by not writing a letter to my friend. Therefore the answer to question 4 is also no. If the answers are no, the probability is high that what I am experiencing is false guilt that should be discarded. But let's take another look.

The answer to question 3, "Is what I did wrong according to God's will or plan for *me?*" could be yes *if* I have a strong sense that God called me to write the letter or if I had made a commitment to do so. Perhaps God wanted me to encourage, confront or share my faith with my friend, and just like Jonah, I went the other way in disobedience. The guilt that I feel, then, would be good because it occurred in response to my disobedience. I should feel guilty because I am guilty.

Let's look some other examples.

Jerry was abused as a child.

1. *Why am I feeling guilty? What did (didn't) I do?* I was abused and I participated. I enjoyed it. I didn't stop it. I let it go on.

Am I responsible? No.

If our answer to the last part of question 1 is no, then we need not continue, because we are not responsible for the thing we are feeling guilty for. Our guilt feelings are false guilt that needs to be shed. Getting rid of guilt like Jerry's may require the assistance of a counselor or support group. *Identifying bad guilt and getting rid of it are not always easy tasks.*

Robin's father died.

1. *Why am I feeling guilty? What did (didn't) I do?* My father died, and I didn't encourage him to go to the doctor sooner.

Am I responsible? Unsure.

2. *Is what I did wrong or sinful according to God's Word (or against the law)?* No.

3. *Is what I did wrong or sinful according to God's plan or will for me?* No.

4. *Is there something I must confess, for which I must ask forgiveness and make amends?* No.

If the answers to questions 2, 3 and 4 are no, then the feelings are most likely based on false or bad guilt.

In another case, if William feels guilty about how he disciplined his son, he might answer the questions like this:

1. *Why am I feeling guilty? What did (didn't) I do?* I got angry at my son and disciplined him too harshly.

Am I responsible? Yes.

2. *Is what I did wrong or sinful according to God's Word?* Yes. Ephesians 6:4 says, "Fathers, do not exasperate your children; instead, bring them up in the training and instruction of the Lord."

3. *Is what I did wrong or sinful accrding to God's plan or will for me?* Yes.

4. *Is there something I must confess, for which I must ask forgiveness and make amends?* Yes.

When any of the answers are in the affirmative, we are generally facing good, godly guilt.

On the other hand, William's situation could be different:

1. *Why am I feeling guilty? What did (didn't) I do?* I got angry at my son and disciplined him for disobeying.

Am I responsible? Yes.

2. *Is what I did wrong or sinful according to God's Word?* No. Hebrews 12:7-9 says, "For what son is not disciplined by his father? If you are not disciplined (and everyone undergoes discipline), then you are illegitimate children and not true sons. Moreover, we have all had human fathers who disciplined us and we respected them for it. How much more should we submit to the Father of our spirits and live!"

3. *Is what I did wrong or sinful according to God's plan or will for me?* No.

4. *Is there something I must confess, for which I must ask forgiveness and make amends?* No.

When the answers are in the negative, we are generally experiencing false guilt.

If Sharon is feeling guilty about engaging in premarital sex, she will find affirmative answers to questions 2, 3 and 4 and know that her feelings are true guilt. If Jim feels guilty about his anger at his co-worker, he may discover his consuming, hateful anger to be sinful. On the other hand, he may feel that his anger has not been hateful or consuming, nor has he let the "sun go down on his anger" (Eph 4:26). He answers questions 2, 3 and 4 in the negative and realizes that he needn't waste time obsessing on this unnecessary guilt but focus on what God wants him to do about the situation.

We use God's Word and his will for us and not our feelings to determine our guilt. Though our feelings help tell us that something is wrong, they are not necessarily accurate, nor do they give reliable testimony of our actual guilt. We must be careful not to rely solely on our guilty *feelings* to convict us of wrongdoing. They must be tested before the Word of God and his personal plan for each of us.

Questions to Help Deal with Bad Guilt

In counseling, Victoria, a single woman in her mid-thirties, confessed, "I used to think that I was supposed to sleep with a guy after a date.

I thought I owed it to him because he had paid for the meal and drinks and dancing. I'd start feeling guilty if I didn't do something for him because he'd done something for me."

"What happened to change it?" I asked.

"I realized that I don't have to feel guilty because I don't really owe him anything. I realized that while I was growing up my mom taught me manners, including the idea that if someone does something nice for you, you should do something nice back. I just took it too far. Now I just tell myself that it is his choice to spend his money that way and I can show my appreciation and be 'nice' in other ways." Victoria identified her guilt and its origin, found her interpretation of it to be flawed and replaced it with a new, healthier perspective.

Later Victoria came to realize that not only had she taken her mother's etiquette "too far," but she no longer agreed that she must always pay back a kindness. When she decided to accept Christ as her Savior and Lord, she began to understand even more what it is like to receive something without ever having to pay for it.

When we find ourselves feeling good guilt, we must confess our sins and receive God's forgiveness. If, however, we discover that we have fallen prey to bad guilt, we need to stop and ask ourselves where our faulty thinking originated. What did we buy into that we shouldn't have? What data needs to be deleted from our conscience's computer program of dos and don'ts or rights and wrongs? We need to ask ourselves a few more questions (see the chart on the next page).

A friend said that he feels guilty if he asks a waiter to have the chef cook his steak a bit longer. When I asked, "Why do you feel guilty? Where does the guilt come from?" he thought for a while and then replied, "When I was little I remember my parents saying that we shouldn't be a bother to other people, that we should always just put up with inconveniences so as not to inconvenience others." I then asked, "Do you agree with that now?" Again he thought for a while. "No, I guess not. Or only in certain situations."

As we displace faulty beliefs, we can replace them with thoughts of God, his promises and the truths in the Word. Perhaps we should also ask ourselves whether Jesus would want us to feel guilty. We can follow the wisdom offered in the timeless story that asks, "What would Jesus do?"

1. Where did this false guilt come from? For example,

☐ Religious legalism?

☐ Societal expectations?

☐ Personal expectations?

☐ Parental or family values and traditions?

☐ Perfectionistic personality?

2. What faulty belief or expectation led to my feeling false guilt? For example,

☐ "I must give to all people all the time whenever asked. It's the Christian thing to do."

☐ "I must be thin and beautiful in order to be accepted and loved."

☐ "I must do whatever my parents ask. I must live up to their expectations for me."

☐ "I must never inconvenience people."

3. What new belief will I put in its place? For example,

☐ "I must seek God for guidance as to who to help."

☐ "God made me and accepts and loves me for who I am."

☐ "I should honor my parents and express appreciation for all they've done for me, but I don't need to feel obligated or guilty for not doing everything they want me to. I do not need to live up to their expectations, but to God's expectations for me."

☐ "I can assert myself and my needs at times as long as I am sensitive to others as well."

Application Questions

1. Think about something you feel guilty for. Ask yourself the questions on page 130 to help distinguish between good and bad guilt.

2. Reflect on an area in which you are experiencing false guilt and ask yourself the questions on page 134 to help deal with bad guilt.

Prayer

Lord, help us distinguish between good and bad guilt so that we may grow closer to you. We want to be obedient to your Word and not responsive to the wrong law and judge. Amen.

FOURTEEN

Dealing with Bad Guilt

W hile writing this book, I momentarily glanced at the bookshelf beside me and was overcome with guilt. I saw books that I feel I should read but haven't gotten around to, a book on regrets and past blunders which reminded me of my own, an oft-neglected Bible and a borrowed book long due back to its owner. This all took place within a few seconds.

Such generally unacknowledged thoughts and feelings can become negative messages I give myself. *Why don't you use your time more wisely so you can read some of those books? Why don't you read your Bible more faithfully? How can you call yourself a professional if you haven't read some of these books? How irresponsible not to return that borrowed book!* Guilt, guilt and more guilt. If I hadn't stopped to reflect, these undesirable messages could have become internalized: *I'm not as competent, godly or responsible as I should be.*

So what must we do to withstand these guilt attacks? How do we stop these marauders? It's not easy, because they are subtle and bombard us constantly.

When we find ourselves stressed, out of sorts, down, dazed, angry, anxious or hurt, we should stop and ask ourselves what's going on. *What is it I'm really feeling?* If we find guilt hiding behind other emotions, we should ask ourselves the four questions given in the last chapter to help us sort out why we are feeling guilty. In order to do this, however, we have to stop midstream and interrupt our inner reflections and obsessions. We may even have to get in tune with our bodies. As I looked at the guilt-producing bookshelf, I noticed I was mentally distracted, my body slouched a bit, and I gave a sigh of disappointment. As I returned to my typing I realized something was amiss, so I stopped and asked the questions. Each time we stop and examine our uncertain or negative feelings and uncover guilt, we build up our defenses against counterproductive, unnecessary guilt.

In response to the question "What advice would you give someone to help them get rid of false guilt?" one person wrote, "I'd tell them to understand the real issues, to determine who's really responsible for any guilt, to recognize their personal limits in the matter and to eliminate false guilt." Another person recommended, "Work at developing a healthy perception of yourself (I am beloved by God, valuable, worthy) and of God and who he is (his grace, forgiveness, how he convicts, his help in standing against temptation)." One person simply responded, "Lose it!"

In the last chapter we sought to improve our ability to identify false guilt. But recognition in and of itself may not be enough. Once the enemy is identified and in view, how do we plan our counterattack? How can we deal with unhealthy guilt in healthy ways? We need not feel helpless; we can take several healthy steps to push back this unwanted visitor.

See Ourselves as God Sees Us

God loves each of us individually. He sent Jesus to die for you and for me. He considers us worthy to be called his children. From God's perspective, we are his forgiven, beloved heirs. He knows our brokenness, imperfections and sinful nature and loves us in spite of it all.

I was fortunate to have heard Corrie ten Boom, the wise and humble survivor of a Nazi concentration camp, speak many years ago. "All too often we tend to see ourselves like this." She lifted up a piece of embroidery, showing us the back side full of loose threads and knots. "But," she continued, "God sees us like this." She then turned the embroidery around to reveal a beautiful and magnificent design. Each thread in its place combined to form an exquisite work of art.

If we focus on the back side of our lives, the one with the loose ends, regrets and mistakes, guilt feelings will overwhelm us like a flood. God wants us to turn the tapestry around, look in the mirror and see the magnificent design he is making in us. My pastor said, "When we're not experiencing God's love, we tend to experience guilt, alienation and insecurity."[1] *We are less likely to fall prey to unnecessary guilt and self-condemnation if we understand how God views us and how much he loves us.*

Know, Be and Accept Ourselves

To *know* ourselves is to look at ourselves honestly and identify what we think, feel, believe and value. It is to acknowledge our preferences and prejudices, biases and bitternesses. To know who we are is to face the reality of our abilities *and* limitations. Knowing who we are is also being aware of our feelings and fears.

To *be* ourselves is to risk rejection by those who think, feel and believe differently. It is to risk the possibility of inviting guilt feelings in, as others may dislike who we are and what we do.

To *accept* ourselves means that we like ourselves in spite of our weaknesses. We don't live a life of regret that focuses on our imperfections.

The more honest we are with ourselves and others, the better we will ward off unnecessary guilt. If we remain closed and fearful of exposure, we can easily fall victim to others' manipulation of our sense of guilt. If we are unable to accept the good, bad and ugly parts of ourselves, bad guilt will trample us. The more self-awareness and self-acceptance we have, the less we fall prey to false guilt.

Admit Our Mistakes

To admit our mistakes is to confront our imperfections, concede our frailties and confess our humanity. Our human nature intuitively seeks to defend rather than admit mistakes. As a result, a lot of unnecessary time and energy is expended and a lot of unnecessary guilt is felt or denied, when the whole mess could have ended with "I was wrong."

Dale Carnegie once said, "When we are wrong—and that will be surprisingly often, if we are honest with ourselves—let's admit our mistakes quickly and with enthusiasm. It is a lot more fun, under the circumstances, than trying to defend one's self."[2] Being willing to admit our mistakes follows closely on the heels of our ability to accept ourselves as imperfect. Once we can accept that reality, admitting mistakes should come a lot more easily. In denying our imperfections and mistakes, we invite the repression or suppression (conscious or subconscious denial) of guilt feelings. Once buried, they are harder to dig out.

Give Up Impossible Dreams

Where expectations abound, disappointment is not far behind, walking hand in hand with guilt feelings. Much of our unnecessary guilt feelings center on our inability to meet our own unrealistic expectations. If we expect too much of ourselves, we welcome guilt feelings into our heart and home. If we expect to be the superspouse, the perfect parent, the envied employee or the fabulous friend, we set ourselves up for a painful fall.

We will never be thin enough, patient enough, smart enough or giving enough. If we buy into these beliefs and expectations we are doomed. Why not openly admit defeat and stop trying to live by unreasonable standards?

A story is told of a conscientious wife who tried very hard to please her ultracritical husband. When she made him a breakfast of scrambled eggs, he'd complain that he'd wanted them poached. If she made them poached, he'd want them scrambled. One morning she decided to prepare one egg each way. Anxiously she awaited his response. He growled, "Can't you do anything right? You've scrambled the wrong one!" For some people, we can't do anything right no matter how hard or how long we try.

The mother of a friend of mine complains that her grown children are never "grateful enough" for all she has done for them. Year after year, my friend has tried to show and convince his mother of his gratitude. He has felt discouraged and deflated. Only when he finally conceded that he could never satisfy his mother's needs could he be free from excessive guilt. He still strives to express appreciation but does not feel incapacitated by his mother's continual comments to the contrary. By admitting defeat, he gained a victory against bad guilt.

Don't Assume What Others Think and Feel

Dennis was sure his wife was upset with him. Even though she didn't say anything, he knew she must be furious. His guilt feelings grew as he worried over how his actions must have hurt her feelings. He became more and more uncommunicative because he felt that no matter what he said, it couldn't convey his remorse.

Jane passed Mark in the corridor at work and said a friendly "hello" but was met with no response. She felt terrible, assuming that she must have done something to offend him. Her guilt feelings soared as she scanned her memories of all their recent encounters.

In both of these instances, the "guilty" party assumed what the other person was thinking or feeling. Dennis assumed his wife was angry but never checked it out with her. Jane assumed Mark was offended at something she had done. In Dennis's case, his wife was unaware of his blunder. And Jane didn't know that Mark had just gotten the news that a close friend was critically ill. He had been oblivious to her presence in the hall because he was preoccupied with his own thoughts.

Often we experience unnecessary guilt feelings because we assume what others are thinking and feeling. We jump to conclusions that leave us overwhelmed with guilt. Rather than assume what someone is thinking or feeling, we need to check it out. If we aren't sure what someone said or meant or did, we should ask for clarification instead of assuming the worst.

Don't Try to Please Everyone All the Time

If we attempt to please everyone, we are going to be surrounded by and overwhelmed with guilt. We want to please our friends, our co-workers, our boss, our spouse, our parents and our children, yet we find it is an impossible task. The more we need others' approval, the more susceptible we will be to their manipulation and wishes—and to bad guilt.

Aesop's fable "The Man and the Donkey" illustrates this point. A man decides to take his donkey to sell at the market. On the way, different people tell him what he should and shouldn't do. Each time he changes as advised. He ends up doing the ridiculous, and loses the donkey. The story concludes, "Please all and you will please none—including yourself."

Deal with Negative Emotions in Positive Ways

Christians frequently feel guilt whenever they experience negative emotions. They believe that they are never to feel angry, sad or impatient. Whenever these emotions appear, they run and hide in the closet of shame.

Jesus displayed anger when he overturned the tables in the temple. Scripture tells us, "In your anger do not sin" (Eph 4:26), indicating that it is okay to be angry or to feel anger, just as long as we do not act out in negative, harmful, sinful ways.

Just read through the Psalms and see how often King David expresses his negative emotions. He openly expresses his frustrations, impatience, concern, anger and ambivalence. Like David, we experience these feelings, yet all too often we feel guilty for having them.

Many Christians also feel guilty when they are not feeling happy. They mistakenly believe rejoicing "in the Lord always" (Phil 4:4) means they must never feel sad or depressed. They put on a happy face, pretending to be content even though they are hurting inside. David's dismay is frequently evident in the Psalms. He feels downtrodden, discouraged and disappointed. He turns to God in his anguish without any sense of shame or embarrassment for his feelings. And in 2 Corinthians 7 Paul admits to "fears within" and being downcast ("depressed," NASB).

If we find ourselves starting to feel guilty over negative emotions, we must stop ourselves and ask if we are being overly restrictive. Are our God-given feelings free, or imprisoned by our guilt?

Reprogram Negative Self-Talk

We need to identify the negative messages we tell ourselves, as I did with the glance at the bookshelf. Once these messages are acknowledged, we can examine them and develop new, healthier ones to replace them. Instead of focusing on negative thoughts and feelings *(I'm not competent, godly or responsible)* I change them in light of God's grace and love *(I will try to be competent at what I do. Though I stumble, I will seek after righteousness. I will return the borrowed book. I am generally a responsible person).*

We can change our thinking and redirect our feelings (referred to by some as cognitive restructuring). When we find ourselves feeling guilty for something, we need not assume the feelings are valid. As we discovered earlier, feelings aren't accurate indicators for determining if we are experiencing good or bad guilt. We must examine and scrutinize the situation by checking to see if we have the facts straight, if we have embraced unrealistic expectations, if we are neglecting to accept our human imperfections, if we have jumped to conclusions and assumptions or if we have been seeing only through our own limited perspective, not through God's.

Remember Our Guilt Game Plan

Remembering and implementing the overall "Guilt Game Plan" will greatly help us in this battle with guilt.

Recognize	the existence and prevalence of guilt
Identify	the sources of guilt
Acknowledge	our ineffective ways of dealing with guilt
Face	guilt and guilty feelings
Distinguish	between good and bad guilt
Eliminate	bad guilt
Respond	to good guilt

Thus far we have worked on developing skills in *recognizing* guilt's presence in our life, since it is often hidden behind other emotions or actions. We have also *identified* where guilt comes from (family, religion, culture, expectations) and *acknowledged* the unhealthy ways we attempt to deal with guilt—masks and disguises, faulty battle plans (fight, flee and surrender), "spiritual" attempts at self-atonement. We have been learning to *face* guilt and to look it in the eyes so that we can better *distinguish* the good from the bad. Once we do that we can begin the process of *eliminating* bad guilt and *responding* appropriately to good guilt.

Pray for Discernment

As we pray, we open ourselves up to the Holy Spirit, who both convicts and comforts us. Praying for discernment means seeking God for wisdom and insight regarding our guilt feelings. It means asking him to expose what's in our hearts and minds, helping us to see the situation more clearly. He can reveal whether our guilt feelings are good or bad.

Application Questions

1. Were you able to identify with the bookshelf example at the beginning of the chapter? Have you experienced a frontal assault of guilt when looking at your desk, sewing room, garage, kitchen or yard? What can you do to better identify and change the guilt attacks?

2. In which of the steps for getting rid of guilt do you feel you need the most work? What can you do to help strengthen that area?

3. What area of the Guilt Game Plan is most difficult for you? Why?

Prayer

Lord, we do need your discernment and your help as we try to get rid of excess guilt. We don't want illegitimate guilt to occupy our hearts and minds—only you. Amen.

FIFTEEN

Conviction & Confession, Not Condemnation

*D*uring a conversation about guilt, JoAnne told me, "When my children were growing up I was a closet alcoholic. When I finally got sober eight years ago, I had to face the fact that I'd been a terrible mom, that I'd been emotionally unavailable for my children. Instead of being ruled by alcohol, I began to be ruled by guilt. By then my children were teenagers. I'd asked for their forgiveness and was trying to be the best mom possible but felt overwhelmed by guilt. It's still hard at times, because my son continually reminds me of how I blew it and tries to use guilt to manipulate me. Fortunately, with God's help, guilt no longer consumes me. In Christ I know I'm forgiven. When I first felt guilty about my past I knew that I was supposed to feel guilty. Now whenever I feel guilty about it I realize that it's not God's conviction but condemnation and that I should let it go."

Conviction is when we sense our true guilt and are led to confession. Condemnation is when we sense needless guilt.

Conviction
The Holy Spirit "will convict the world of guilt in regard to sin and

righteousness and judgment. . . . The Spirit . . . will guide you into all truth" (Jn 16:8, 13). The Holy Spirit

> is the Author, Source, and Director of power for the lifelong process of spiritual growth, and it is only as He is the sphere of the believer's walk that victory over sin is possible. Setting the saint free from a stringent, legalistic clinging to the letter of the law, the Spirit is the Spirit of Christ the Liberator, and the Transformer of the sinner, bringing him into conformity with the image of Christ (2 Cor 3:17).[1]

Conviction usually comes with an uneasiness in our spirit. It may come through our knowledge of God's Word, through our conscience, or through others' words or deeds. Knowing *God's Word* will help us know when we have wandered from his way. The Bible reveals God's plans and desires for us as well as those things he despises and considers ungodly. The Holy Spirit also uses our *conscience*, our heart and mind, to instill a sense of wrongdoing. When we sense in our spirit that something is wrong, it is often the Holy Spirit letting us know that we are straying from the desired path. The Holy Spirit also uses *people* to convict us, by either their words or example.

The author of *How to Live with Your Feelings* writes, "A sense of conscience, a feeling of conviction, or a feeling of guilt which occurs as a result of true biblical sin (godly sorrow) is like a sense of pain, unpleasant but helpful in telling us that something is amiss. As part of the ministry of the Holy Spirit, such feelings, honestly confronted, can then be examined in light of Scripture."[2]

We must be receptive to the conviction of the Holy Spirit to help us discern when we should and shouldn't feel guilty. If we are sensitive to godly conviction and not worldly condemnation, we will improve our ability to distinguish between good and bad guilt.

What Conviction Requires

A man was saying good night to his son. Kneeling beside the bed, the little boy prayed, "Lord, I'm sorry that I disobeyed you today. Please forgive me. Help me to grow up to be a wise man like Daddy." Later that night, the father reflected in prayer, "Lord, I'm sorry that I disobeyed you today. Please forgive me. Help me to be childlike and humble, like my son."

Conviction requires a soft heart, a humble spirit and a listening ear, like those of this father and son. Without a *soft heart* that is aware of its guilty, sin-ridden nature and is receptive to God, we will miss many opportunities to grow in godliness through the conviction and pruning of the Holy Spirit.

I have heard it said that Christians "must have a tough skin to the ways of the world and a tender heart to the ways of the Lord." We frequently get these reversed when we allow our skin to be tender to the judgment of people. "The judgment of people" refers to the expectations, fads and norms that society places on us as well as our own self-imposed judgments. These generally bring condemnation, distracting us from a loving, forgiving God. At the same time, we often allow our hearts to become tough and unreceptive to the conviction and guidance of the Holy Spirit. We let the world get under our skin and let our tough hearts keep the Comforter at a distance.

Proverbs 4:23 warns us, "Above all else, guard your heart, for it is the wellspring of life." In order to be receptive to the conviction of the Holy Spirit, we must guard our hearts. We must watch for infiltration by the enemy, who wants us to have hard hearts that are insensitive to God. Satan wants our hearts to be either full of pride and defensiveness or overly sensitive, easily guilt-ridden and indiscriminate. Satan doesn't want us to develop discernment or to have tender, God-centered hearts.

Those who love gardening know that the best way to dislodge an unwanted weed is to soften the soil around it, and the best way to soften the soil is with moisture. We must let the Holy Spirit be the One to remove the weeds from the garden of our lives. And the best way to make our hearts more receptive to God's weeding is through our tears of repentance.

When we are confronted with our sin and there's nowhere to run and hide, we can either soften our hearts by admitting our wrong or become hardhearted and deny any wrongdoing. In this book I have discussed battle plans, strategies and tactics for gaining a victory over guilt. When all is said and done, perhaps our best defense is to have a heart that is readily accessible to the conviction of the Holy Spirit and unwavering in confession.

Scripture also repeatedly reminds us to be *humble* (Jas 4:10; 1 Pet

5:6). If we strive to be humble in spirit, we are more receptive to God's guidance and to the conviction of the Holy Spirit. "He guides the humble in what is right and teaches them his way" (Ps 25:9). It is difficult for us to learn if we remain prideful and hardhearted. "This is the one I esteem: he who is humble and contrite in spirit, and trembles at my word" (Is 66:2).

Without a *listening ear,* we will also be unable to hear or receive the necessary conviction for our wrongdoings. To listen, we must "be still, and know that I am God" (Ps 46:10). By acknowledging who he is, we begin to understand his sovereignty and our humanity, his greatness and our lowly state. Amidst our feelings of insignificance, we realize his significance and become more attuned to his voice, his calling, his wisdom and his guidance. Gaining the right perspective on his majesty helps us to be better listeners as we learn to wait on him, allowing him to speak to our tender, humble hearts.

When we are overwhelmed with feelings of inadequacy, we need to ask God to give us a heart that is tender, a spirit of humility and an ear that hears his voice. Conviction could be viewed as someone knocking at the door of our heart. In order to open the door, our hearts must be receptive, discerning and welcoming. We must keep the door unlocked so that the Holy Spirit can enter. We must be cautious, however, not to open the door to every thought that knocks, as we may allow false guilt to enter. But how do we tell the difference? How do we know when to shut out the judgment of people and when to open the door to the judgment (conviction) of God?

Discernment

Discernment requires that we develop the ability to differentiate whether our sense of wrongdoing is from God or from people. Unfortunately, our tendency toward rationalization and self-justification often gets in the way. We lose sight of what is from God when we concentrate our efforts on self-preservation and protection. We need to allow God freer access to our hearts by laying down our lives before him.

How can we maximize our ability to set ourselves aside and listen to God? Here are several suggestions.

1. *Seek God.* When faced with a sense of wrongdoing, draw near

to God. Spend time in praise and worship, remembering who he is and who you are in light of his presence and majesty.

2. *Read his Word.* Knowing God's Word will help you understand and know his ways. "The statutes of the LORD are trustworthy, making wise the simple" (Ps 19:7). "Your word is a lamp to my feet and a light for my path" (Ps 119:105). The Bible is our life's manual.

3. *Pray.* Pray for clarity, guidance, wisdom, direction. Ask God to help reveal the origin of your sense of wrongdoing. Pray earnestly that God would confirm the wrongdoing with conviction from the Holy Spirit *or* expose the feelings and thoughts as originating from the father of lies (Jn 8:44).

4. *Seek godly advisers.* God often speaks through those around us. Proverbs tells us, "Listen to advice and accept instruction, and in the end you will be wise" (19:20). The advice of godly counselors can help you be wise and victorious (Prov 11:14) in your efforts to distinguish what is from God from what is not.

Pitfalls to Discernment

You may find yourself thinking, *Hearing God's voice and discerning what is and isn't from him is too hard.* Sometimes our biggest stumbling block is ourselves. While seeking discernment we must fight against the many ways our fallen nature obstructs God's workings. When I was confronted by a colleague, I focused on the part of his message that was untrue. I felt justified in my crusade against his unfair accusations. While the message was partially incorrect, it was also partially correct. He did pinpoint some areas in my life that needed improvement. It took a while before I was willing to take a good hard look at those sinful areas in my life. I wanted to focus on where my colleague was incorrect, not where he hit the bull's-eye.

When confronted, we must guard against our tendency to disregard the message if the messenger or the way the message is presented is faulty. God can use anyone and any means to reveal our misdeeds to us. We must also beware of our tendency to focus on inaccuracies rather than the truth.

Discernment requires an ability to distinguish between what is and isn't of God. Unfortunately it isn't always clear-cut, one hundred percent, all or nothing. When we sense a wrongdoing or are confronted, we must be careful not to throw the good out with the bad. We must be diligent to determine what, if anything, God wants us to deal with. Even faulty accusations generally contain partial truth, and it is our job to identify it.

In addition to watching out for defensiveness, we must guard against our tendency to want to resolve concerns too quickly. A friend told me that whenever she is confronted by other Christians, she immediately thinks they are right and that what they share is from God "because I assume their relationship with God is stronger than mine." She sees no need for discernment, only full acceptance. We may prematurely assume that we are guilty without spending the time to discern the true source of the judgment, and we may incorrectly discount the the conviction of the Holy Spirit. We must be patient, letting the Holy Spirit speak to our hearts.

Condemnation

Without discernment, we fall prey to the judgment of this world and become trapped in a vicious cycle of false guilt and condemnation. Whenever we feel condemnation and guilt, it is highly likely that the standards by which we are judging ourselves are not of God. The world tends to condemn the sinner as well as the sin. God *convicts* the sinner and *condemns* the sin. "God . . . condemned sin in sinful man" (Rom 8:3).

As Christians we are no longer imprisoned by the condemnation of the world. Paul declares, "There is now no condemnation for those who are in Christ Jesus, because through Christ Jesus the law of the Spirit of life set me free from the law of sin and death" (Rom 8:1-2).

Jordan was caught in a cycle of condemnation that seemed unbreakable. We talked about God's love and forgiveness and identified the underlying negative messages and faulty beliefs, but an overwhelming sense of failure lingered. In one of our sessions, as we prayed for God's power to break through, I sensed that I was supposed to share a story from my own life in which I had similarly struggled. I explained how God had broken through my fortified barriers of self-condemnation and pride with his love and forgiveness. As I spoke, Jordan's eyes got a bit watery. "I thought I was the only one who struggled with feelings of failure and self-condemnation and most Christians never had to deal with it. I thought that no one could get free from it and there was no hope for me."

Condemnation is counterproductive. It keeps us from experiencing the "joy of the Lord" (Neh 8:10). Breaking through can be hard and may require the help of a pastor, mature Christian or Christian counselor. For Jordan, change began with the realization that others have had similar struggles *and* were able to break free.

Repentance

The outcome of the conviction of the Holy Spirit should be a "broken and contrite heart" (Ps 51:17). When King David was overcome with sin, he repented: "For I know my transgressions, and my sin is always before me" (Ps 51:3). The recognition of our sin should drive us to repentance and draw us to God. One author states it well: "Guilt is only a virtue if it leads to repentance and newness of relationship with Christ. After that it usually serves no godly purpose."[3] Repentance involves both recognition of and remorse over our sins.

In 2 Corinthians 7:10 we read, "Godly sorrow brings repentance that leads to salvation and leaves no regret, but worldly sorrow brings death." This verse illustrates our two possible responses to the conviction of guilt. The first response is *godly sorrow*, a God-focused sorrow that leads to repentance—a deep remorse accompanied by a desire to discontinue the sinful behavior. The second response is *worldly sorrow*, a self-centered sorrow that focuses on self-atonement, the consequences of our sin and the removal of the emotional pain.

Worldly sorrow concerns itself more with how to feel better and how to get rid of the guilt feelings than on how to be restored to unbroken fellowship with God. It is fueled by our fears (of punishment, abandonment and inadequacy).

Godly sorrow can be thought of as a God-focused process that leads to repentance, confession, forgiveness and spiritual life. Whereas worldly sorrow seeks to free itself from uncomfortable guilt feelings, godly sorrow, in a sense, seeks to increases our pain so that we will sin less. As we fully experience the depth of our sin, we will be less inclined to sin again in the future. Perhaps those of us in the counseling profession should be less intent on helping people to feel better at times when they should more fully experience the pain of their sin.

"When a human being considers the . . . stray places to which his heart runs, the failures that have marked him in the year past, it is time first to weep. From remorse, a person can lose the motivation to sin. Through feelings—feelings of guilt that lead to remorse—a person can be renewed."[4] True repentance occurs when we experience true godly sorrow.

My brother, who is a pastor, views worldly sorrow as the unrepentant heart that grieves over the consequences of the sin rather than the sin itself. He cited Cain as an example. "Now Cain said to his brother Abel, 'Let's go out to the field.' And while they were in the field, Cain attacked his brother Abel and killed him. Then the LORD said to Cain, 'Where is your brother Abel?' 'I don't know," he replied. 'Am I my brother's keeper?' . . . Cain said to the LORD 'My punishment is more than I can bear' " (Gen 4:8-9, 13). Cain grieved over the consequences he faced as a result of the sin, not the sin itself.

My brother went on to say, "Godly sorrow, on the other hand, occurs when we grieve over the sin itself." We see this kind of repentance in David's confession in Psalm 51:

Against you, you only, have I sinned
  and done what is evil in your sight,
so that you are proved right when you speak
  and justified when you judge. . . .
Create in me a pure heart, O God,
  and renew a steadfast spirit within me. (vv. 4, 10)

David was truly repentant, grieving deeply over the sins he committed. He was more distraught over the broken relationship with God that his sin caused than he was with the consequences of that sin. Like David we should grieve not only because we have sinned but also because our sin comes between us and God.

B. B. Warfield, the respected Princeton theologian of the late 1800s and early 1900s, wrote in reference to the Greek word used for repentance *(metamelomai)* in 2 Corinthians 7, "Here it prevailing stands for that fundamental change of mind by which the back is turned not upon one sin or some sins, but upon all sin, and the face definitely turned to God and to His service."[5]

Second Corinthians 7:11 tells of the benefits we gain from godly sorrow: "See what this godly sorrow has produced in you: what earnestness, what eagerness to clear yourselves, what indignation, what alarm, what longing, what concern, what readiness to see justice done."

Let's look at another biblical comparison, this time between Peter and Judas. When Peter faced his guilt of denying his Lord Jesus Christ three times, he responded with a deep sense of remorse. Why? Because his sin came between him and his Lord. This sorrow led him to a repentance that resulted in an even deeper relationship with his Lord and Savior. On the other hand, when Judas faced his guilt of betraying Jesus, he responded by returning the money he received for his deed, trying to redeem himself. His self-focused sorrow was accompanied by regret rather than repentance. Colin Brown writes, "Judas recognized that Jesus had been wrongly condemned. He regretted his betrayal (Matt. 27:3), but he did not find the way to genuine repentance."[6]

Repentance means a *changing of our mind*, from a self-centered to

2 Corinthians 7:10
Our Responses to Guilt

Godly sorrow involves	*Worldly sorrow involves*
God-focus	Self-focus
Conviction	Condemnation
Remorse (over sin and broken relationship with God)	Regret or remorse (over consequences of sin)
Attitude: dependence, Christ paid	Attitude: autonomy, I'll pay
Motivation for change: love	Motivation for change: get rid of guilt feelings
which leads to	*which leads to*
Repentance Forgiveness Salvation Spiritual life	Spiritual death
Examples	*Examples*
David (Ps 51) Peter (Mt 26:69-75)	Cain (Gen 4) Judas (Mt 27:1-10)

a God-centered perspective. It doesn't just imply a turning around but a transformation and renewing of our mind and attitude. It implies awareness and acknowledgment of our guilt and guilty nature. As we repent, we face our sins rather than hide from them. When Jesus enlarged the scope of our guilt and sin, he proclaimed even our thoughts and emotions as capable of sin. He pronounces us guilty of murder if we harbor anger and guilty of adultery if we entertain lustful thoughts. So our repentance must encompass deeds, thoughts and emotions.

Repentance also includes a *commitment to change.* This change involves our willingness to make restitution and to reconcile as needed. "When a man or woman wrongs another in any way and so is unfaithful to the LORD, that person is guilty and must confess the sin he has committed. He must make full restitution for his wrong, add one fifth to it and give it all to the person he has wronged" (Num 5:6-7). Robert South wrote, "Repentance has a double aspect; it looks upon things past with a weeping eye, and upon the future with a watchful eye." Without restitution and earnest attempts to change, repentance becomes meaningless and empty. Paul encouraged believers to "prove their repentance by their deeds" (Acts 26:20).

Repentance involves	
recognition	of our guilt
remorse	over our sin
renunciation	of our sin
reconciliation	to God and to the person(s) offended
restoration	to a right relationship with God and others
restitution	for our sin
Repentance requires	
conviction	remorse over our sinful deeds
confession	(private or public)
change	from past sinful words, thoughts or misdeeds
commitment	to make amends and to strive for godliness

Jeremiah records God's wonderful promise: "If you repent, I will restore you" (Jer 15:19).

Confession

"I *confess* my iniquity; I am troubled by my sin" (Ps 38:18). As we become troubled by our sin, we are drawn to confess our sinfulness before God. One of the key steps in the twelve-step Alcoholics Anonymous program requires that the individual confess his or her wrongs. This important step requires humility, honesty and vulnerability. Interestingly, it is those who disregard this step who are most prone to fall back into alcohol abuse. Proverbs tells us, "He who conceals his sins does not prosper, but whoever confesses and renounces them finds mercy" (28:13).

Confession requires surrendering ourselves to God and his plan for cleansing and restoration. "Confessing one's sins to God and receiving divine forgiveness is not cheap and easy; on the contrary, it requires surrender."[7] This surrender brings captivity for the sin but freedom for the sinner—freedom from guilt.

When we surrender our guilt and confess our sin to God, they lose power over us. Regarding confession, Dietrich Bonhoeffer writes, "The expressed, acknowledged sin has lost all its power. It has been revealed and judged as sin. He is no longer alone with his evil for he has cast off his sin in confession and handed it over to God. It has been taken away from him."[8]

> What would have happened if Eve had said to Adam and to God—"I really want to eat this fruit. Help me, I'm struggling." We don't know. However, we are told that hiding it didn't help. In contrast, the New Testament says that we should confess our faults to one another. That is, we should come out of hiding. False guilt—or any guilt—is a call to confession.[9]

Confession must be a response of the heart, not a duty of the mind. To confess in a mechanical way is to defy the true meaning of confession, an outpouring of the sinful heart before a forgiving God. "Let him guard against ever making a pious work of his confession. If he does so it will become the final, most abominable, vicious, and impure prostitution of the heart; the act becomes an idle, lustful babbling. Confession as a routine duty is spiritual death."[10]

Confession requires a willingness to admit not only our guilty nature but also our specific guilty acts, thoughts and feelings. We confess our sinful nature, which *kept* us apart from God, as well as our sinful acts, which *keep* us apart from God. "Lord, forgive my sinful heart" must be accompanied by the admission of our specific sins: "Lord, forgive me for the ways in which I have been prideful with Kim, insensitive to Dawn and unforgiving of Shari, when I . . ." Just as gossips give all the juicy details, so should we in our confessions.

Confession is generally made in three ways: (1) secret confession to God, (2) private confession to the one offended and (3) public confession to the church or to a trusted community of people (support, accountability or fellowship group). James encourages us, "Confess to one another therefore your faults—your slips, your false steps, your offenses, your sins; and pray for one another, that you may be healed and restored—to a spiritual tone of mind and heart" (Jas 5:16 Amplified).

When I asked God to reveal areas of needed confession in my life, he brought the names of several people by whom I felt offended. I thought that perhaps God didn't understand my request—I had asked him to show me where I needed to confess, not where I needed to forgive those who had wronged me. But God was calling me to confess and to ask forgiveness from those to whom I felt I should be granting forgiveness. I began to realize that I had turned wrongs done to me into wrongs that I was committing. He showed me that my sins of lingering anger, dislike and an unforgiving spirit far surpassed others' initial offense. So not only did I confess my sins before God, but I also felt God wanted me to confess my sins to some of these people. It was quite a humbling experience to ask forgiveness from someone who had offended me and to realize that my sinful attitude toward them was of more concern to God than their wrong to me.

Ask God to show you areas in your life that you need to change and confess. Ask him to bring to mind names of those to whom you need to make confession. Bonhoeffer encourages us to follow the admonition of James:

Confession in the presence of a brother is the profoundest kind of humiliation. It hurts, it cuts a man down, it is a dreadful blow to pride. To stand there before a brother as a sinner is an ignominity that is almost unbearable. In the confession of concrete sins the old man dies a painful, shameful death before the eyes of a brother. As long as I am by myself in the confession of my sins everything remains in the dark, but in the presence of a brother the sin has to be brought into the light.[11]

Richard Foster adds, "God has given us our brothers and sisters to stand in Christ's stead and make God's presence and forgiveness real to us."[12] Confession breaks the cycle of condemnation and guilt.

God's Plan

God offers forgiveness and freedom while the enemy of our souls offers an endless cycle of false guilt and condemnation.

God's Plan	Satan's Plan
We feel convicted	We feel condemned
The Holy Spirit confirms the "sin"	The world confirms the "sin"
We experience true guilt	We experience false guilt
We feel remorse, sorrow, repentance	We feel anger, rebellion, shame or despair
We repent	We flee, fight or surrender
We confess	We fall prey to repeating this cycle over and over because we don't face guilt, don't examine its source or aren't remorseful
We receive forgiveness and freedom	We remain in bondage to false guilt

Earl Wilson writes,

> David premeditated adultery and murder. . . . [He had] periods of remorse and soul-searching repentance as is evidenced in Psalm 51. He was a broken man. BUT he did not stay broken. He was lifted up by God. . . . What was his secret? Psalm 32:4, 5: "I acknowledged my sin to You and did not cover up my iniquity . . . and You forgave the guilt of my sin." David's . . . response was to go back to God and start over. . . . He acknowledged it all. God's response was not only to forgive the transgressions but also to deal with the guilt. . . . God restored David in terms of both the legal and the emotional aspects of guilt. Restoration cannot take place until the crippling aspects of guilt are gone.[13]

Like David, we can rejoice that both our sin and the guilt of our sin are forgiven. When we confess our sins, we are freed from those things that have kept us from God—free to commune with a God who is faithful, just and forgiving. "If we confess our sins, he is faithful and just and will forgive us our sins and purify us from all unrighteousness" (1 Jn 1:9).

Application Questions
1. In what ways and in what areas have you experienced conviction?
2. What do you need to improve your ability to receive conviction? In which area are you weakest: having a soft heart, a humble spirit or a listening ear?
3. In what ways can you increase your ability to discern God's conviction from human condemnation? What "pitfalls" do you stumble into?
4. Is there something you need to confess and repent of?

Prayer
Lord, please help us to have a tender heart and a humble spirit that listen to you. Help us to be sensitive to the conviction of the Holy Spirit while not falling prey to the condemnation of this world. When we sin, we want to respond with godly and not worldly sorrow. Reveal to us what we need to confess before you and before others. Amen.

S I X T E E N

Forgiveness & Freedom

*W*hen Gary came in for counseling, he was extremely guilt-ridden because of frequent relapses into compulsive addictions. He knew that he was supposed to ask for forgiveness, but he thought that God's forgiveness only goes so far, that he had long surpassed his quota and that somehow he was supposed to do something in exchange for the forgiveness.

Once a little boy wanted to buy the Washington Monument. He told a guard that he had thirty-four cents and wanted to buy it. The man replied, "You need to understand three things. First, thirty-four cents or thirty-four million dollars is not enough to buy the Washington Monument. Second, it is not for sale. And third, if you are an American citizen, the Washington Monument already belongs to you."

Forgiveness is much the same. First, we cannot earn it. No amount of service, ministry, works, faith, repentance or confession can earn it or pay for it. Second, forgiveness is not for sale. And third, through Christ forgiveness already has been given to us. As Gary began to comprehend the free, continual and unconditional nature of forgiveness, he was able to incorporate it into his life. Horace Bushnell referred to forgiveness as "man's deepest need and God's highest achievement." One woman said, "I used to be motivated by guilt, but as I understand more about God's love and forgiveness, I find myself motivated more and more by love, not guilt."

The Gift

Forgiveness is a gift from God, not something we can earn or buy or ever deserve. God forgives us because of who he is, not because of who we are or what we have done. Just as there is nothing we can do to rid ourselves of our guilty nature, there is nothing we can do to earn God's forgiveness. He knows that our sinful nature is in desperate need of cleansing and forgiveness.

When we acknowledge our sin before God, confessing our transgressions, we find pardon rather than the harsh sentence we deserve. David wrote, "Then I acknowledged my sin to you and did not cover up my iniquity . . . and you forgave the guilt of my sin" (Ps 32:5).

God's forgiveness is freely available to *all* of us. "This righteousness from God comes through faith in Jesus Christ to all who believe. There is no difference, for all have sinned and fall short of the glory of God, and are justified freely by his grace through the redemption that came by Christ Jesus. God presented him as a sacrifice of atonement" (Rom 3:22-25). We are justified freely because Jesus paid the sacrificial price for us all.

This gift brings healing to our deep emotional hurts, relief from our sin-enslaved lives and freedom from obsession with guilt. John Gilmore writes, "The most powerful therapeutic idea in the world is the realization of God's forgiveness."[1] Psalm 103 admonishes us to remember the many benefits that come from knowing God. Among those listed, the first and perhaps foremost is that God "forgives all your sins" (v. 3). What a wondrous benefit!

God doesn't forgive us because we're good. He forgives us because he's good.

The High Price

Picture yourself before a just judge who declares you undeniably "guilty." As you await sentencing, you discover that someone has stepped forward and offered to take your punishment. The judge agrees to the substitution, then turns and announces that you are pardoned, free to go. Jesus is the One who stood in our place, taking the penalty that we deserve. He paid the price for our sins to be forgiven. He was our sin offering (Rom 8:3) and our atoning sacrifice: "Jesus Christ, the Righteous One. He is the atoning sacrifice for our sins, and not only for ours but also for the sins of the whole world" (1 Jn 2:1-2).

We must not take forgiveness for granted. God paid a high price for it. God took our sins and nailed them on the cross with Jesus. Jesus' death brought life to us who were dead in our sins—it brought forgiveness. God made the ultimate sacrifice, sending his only Son to die for our sins that we might have life (Jn 3:16). "When you were dead in your sins and in . . . your sinful nature, God . . . forgave us all our sins. . . . He took it away, nailing it to the cross" (Col 2:13-14).

The Assurances

Though we sin, God won't desert us. Scripture tells us that God won't abandon us even though we continually stumble and fall. No matter what we do, he won't reject us or turn away. His forgiveness is given to all who ask.

In Jeremiah we're told that though the "land is full of guilt," the people "have not been forsaken by their God, the LORD Almighty" (51:5). In Nehemiah, "Our forefathers became arrogant and stiffnecked, and did not obey your commands. . . . But you are a forgiving God, gracious and compassionate, slow to anger and abounding in love. Therefore you did not desert them" (9:16-17).

We can count on God's faithfulness to forgive. If we confess our sins God promises to be faithful to forgive us and to purify or cleanse us from unrighteousness (1 Jn 1:9). In this Scripture

> cleanses [*purifies* in the NIV] is in a continuous tense. It refers not to a once-for-all cleansing, but to an activity which takes place day by day. . . . Sin is something that persists. It clings to the sinner. . . . Of those who confess their sins (the plural is significant: we confess specific sins not simply that we sin). . . . God is "faithful and just"; he forgives. He can be thoroughly relied upon.[2]

We needn't worry that God's forgiveness is situational or intermittent.

His pardon for our sins can be relied on time after time after time. We can depend on him because he is faithful, consistent and trustworthy.

God's forgiveness is personal. In Mark 16 we read of Jesus' resurrection. When the women went to the tomb they were told, "Go, tell his disciples and Peter, 'He is going ahead of you into Galilee' " (v. 7). The women were instructed to tell the disciples *and Peter.* Peter had denied knowing Christ Jesus and might have considered himself excluded because of his guilt. Jesus knew this and made a point of including him by name—just as he does with us. Our guilt can make us feel alienated from God. He wants us to know, just as he wanted Peter to know, that we're forgiven, beloved and called by name. "But now, this is what the LORD says . . . 'Fear not, for I have redeemed you; I have summoned you by name; you are mine' " (Is 43:1).

We can look to the future with hope. Forgiveness allows us to move on in the midst of our imperfections. The weight of our sins brings despair, but the wonder of forgiveness brings hope. We deserve God's fury but receive his favor; we deserve the penalty for our sins but instead receive compassion. "He does not treat us as our sins deserve or repay us according to our iniquities" (Ps 103:10).

Rather than be immobilized by our sins, we can cast them at Jesus' feet, knowing that he will carry them for us. When we have confessed our sins and received forgiveness, we are free to fly unencumbered by our forgiven, cleansed guilt. Eugene de Guerin said, "When the soul has laid down its faults at the feet of God, it feels as though it had wings."

Our sins are far removed. God's Word tells us that our sins are taken far away: "As far as the east is from the west, so far has he removed our transgressions from us" (Ps 103:12). We don't have to face our blunders, for they have been banished out of sight.

Our sins are not held against us. God does not keep track of our sins but permanently erases the score sheet. "Blessed is the man whose sin the LORD does not count against him" (Ps 32:2).

The story was told of a priest who understood God's forgiveness but struggled with appropriating it for a particular sin of his past for which he was extremely remorseful. A woman came to see the priest and claimed to have visions in which she spoke directly with Christ. The priest was skeptical and told the woman to ask God what sin he had committed during his younger years. When she returned several days later telling of another visit from Christ, the priest asked, "Did you ask him what sin I committed in my past?"

She answered, "Yes, I asked him."

"Well, what did he say?"

"He said, 'I don't remember.' "

The Comprehensive Cleansing

Not only is God's forgiveness free, it is also complete. There is no need to supplement what he has done or seek other means to cleanse ourselves. He does a thorough job.

God has the only proven-effective remover for our guilt-stained lives (Jer 2:22). Though our sins are "like scarlet," he will make them as "white as snow" (Is 1:18). David asks, "Cleanse me . . . and I will be clean; wash me, and I will be whiter than snow" (Ps 51:7).

Jesus' final sacrifice not only takes away our sins but also provides a means through which we are transformed inside and out. The forgiveness we have in Jesus cleanses not only our sins but our consciences as well. Hebrews tell us, "How much more, then, will the blood of Christ . . . cleanse our consciences" (9:14). The pervasiveness of our sin requires a comprehensive forgiveness plan that not only includes our deeds but goes deeper to our thoughts, feelings and motivations.

In Jesus we have a complete redemption plan. Psalm 130 proclaims, "But with you there is forgiveness. . . . With the Lord is unfailing love and with him is *full* redemption" (vv. 4, 7). God's forgiveness is effective, comprehensive *and* accompanied by his unfailing love.

Transformation and New Identity

Forgiveness in the Old Testament was temporary and external, obtained through sacrifices to God. But Jesus' ultimate sacrifice brought forgiveness that is permanent and internal. Along with forgiveness, "inwardly we are being renewed day by day" (2 Cor 4:16). The work of forgiveness happens the moment we turn to God, while the work of the indwelling Holy Spirit helps in the transformation process. "We . . . are being transformed into his likeness with ever-increasing glory, which comes from the Lord, who is the Spirit" (2 Cor 3:18). We have forgiveness of sins *and* assistance with the transformation and renewal process.

Jesus' death provides the means through which we are given a new identity. We are no longer wretched sinners but beloved children, no longer strangers and aliens but friends and fellow-citizens (Jn 1:12; 15:14; Eph 2:19).

Unfortunately, many Christians live as if their forgiveness had been obtained the Old Testament way—as if it were temporary and external. They walk around motivated more by guilt than by hope. They live in fear of sin rather than free in Christ. They need to adopt their new identity.

A thought-provoking friend who is a pastor reflected, "The cross removes our guilt, and because of the cross, our new identity removes our shame. The forgiveness offered through Jesus offers us much more than the removal of our sins; it offers us freedom from our sinful identity and offers us the power available for the transformation into our new identity."[3]

Obstacles to Freedom

God desires that we experience the freedom that accompanies forgiveness. Too often, however, we encounter obstacles that prevent us from fully accepting his gift. Galatians 5:1 tells us, "It is for freedom that Christ has set us free. Stand firm, then, and do not let yourselves be burdened again by a yoke of slavery." Our "slavery" is perhaps those obstacles that keep us from experiencing God's forgiveness. Why do we remain enslaved to sin rather than live free in forgiveness?

We don't open the gift. Forgiveness leads to freedom *if* we appropriate it into our lives. If we ask for forgiveness yet do not personally embrace it, it is as if we are holding a beautiful present that we never open. Some of us are hesitant to open the gift because we feel undeserving. Others of us want to do things for God, to somehow "pay" for the gift. It is often hard for us to accept something that has no strings attached. But in order to experience freedom from guilt, we must open God's gift of forgiveness.

We get stuck with regrets. Earlier we discussed the difference between godly and worldly sorrow in 2 Corinthians 7:10. This verse also informs us that our repentance should "leave no regret." Recognition of our sin before God brings remorse and repentance, which should lead to renunciation, restitution, reconciliation and restoration—*not* regret.

Regrets can paralyze us so that we are unable to move on to repentance and fully accept God's forgiveness. To wallow in our sin, to wish over and over and over again that we could change the past, only serves to hinder our full acceptance of God's forgiveness. Regrets keep us in bondage to our sin and the past, whereas remorse encourages us toward changed behavior in the present and future.

Why do we act like pigs that when bathed and cleaned return immediately to the mud? We are told that God picks us up out of the mud and mire and sets our feet on a firm place (Ps 40:2). When we slip into the mud and mire of our sins and God helps us out, we should stay out. Paul encourages us by his example: "Forgetting what is behind and straining toward what is ahead, I press on" (Phil 3:13-14). Rather than be pressured by our past, let's press on.

We don't forgive ourselves. A man in his mid-fifties said of an incident that had happened over two decades earlier, "I know God forgives me; I just can't forgive myself." When we don't forgive ourselves we cling to our sins instead of releasing them to God so he can take them far, far away.

Many years ago when I heard the late Corrie ten Boom speak, she said that when God forgives us, he takes our sins to the deepest part of the ocean, attaches a large weight, drops them overboard and puts up a "No Fishing" sign. All too frequently, she said, we get out our fishing poles and go looking for our sins because we're not ready or willing to give them up—we haven't forgiven ourselves.

Forgiving ourselves may be one of the toughest jobs we encounter. It is difficult to move past our faults to God's forgiveness. We sin and are saddened, we remember and regret. Our godly sorrow is experienced as badness instead of sadness. When we cling to past, forgiven sins, we turn good guilt into bad guilt and respond more with self-centered worldly sorrow than with God-focused godly sorrow.

We feel our sin is too great. John White tells of an experience he had with a man named Howard, who was diagnosed as suffering from psychotic depression. One day they got on the topic of forgiveness. Howard said, "I want it so *bad* . . . but I'm too bad for that. . . . I don't deserve ever to be forgiven." To this White replied, "You're darn right you don't!"

Many of us, like Howard, continually struggle with our sin, feeling undeserving of God's forgiveness. We view our sin as too atrocious, disgraceful, grievous, dreadful and despicable for even God to forgive. We don't deserve God's favor and never will. But by definition forgiveness is never deserved. Until we realize the depth of God's unconditional forgiveness, we will remain in the depths of despair, never able to experience the freedom that comes with God's full pardon.

White writes,

I found my anger increasing. "And who d'you think you are to say Christ's death was not enough for you? Who are you to feel you must add your miserable pittance to the great gift God offers you? Is his sacrifice not good enough for the likes of you?" . . . Suddenly he [Howard] began both to cry and to pray at once . . . "God, I'm real sorry. I didn't mean to offend you. . . . I don't know how to say it. Thank you. . . . Gee, God, *thank you.*"

White informs us that Howard made "remarkable improvement," was taken off medication and was soon released from the hospital.[4] For Howard, understanding and appropriating the all-inclusiveness of God's forgiveness was the key to his emotional well-being. *God's forgiveness is greater than our sin.*

Remembering Our Sins

Once in college I took something and never returned it. Guilt haunted me for years. I confessed my sin before God and made amends but continued to feel guilty. Whenever I recalled my sinful deed I was overcome with guilt. God had made it clear that I'd been forgiven. Remembering my past sins was wrong, because God had called me to move on, forgiven and free. My guilt feelings, originally based on good guilt, had become bad guilt because I was hanging on to forgiven sin.

How can we fully accept God's forgiveness when our minds still recall our sinful deeds? Are we allowing bad guilt a stronghold when we dwell on our past, forgiven sins?

Peter Holdaas, a pastor, once told me that Paul's references to his preconversion sins provide a model to help us understand how to deal with our memories. Paul writes,

For I am the least of the apostles and do not even deserve to be called an apostle, because I persecuted the church of God. (1 Cor 15:9)

Although I am less than the least of all God's people, this grace
was given me. (Eph 3:8)

Christ Jesus came into the world to save sinners—of whom I am
the worst. (1 Tim 1:15)

Paul's references to his former sins and to being the "least" and the
"worst" may demonstrate the difficulty we all experience in self-for-
giveness. More likely, however, they demonstrate his remembrance of
the greatness of God's grace to him. In recalling the depth of his sin,
Paul simultaneously remembers the depth of God's love and forgiveness. Like Paul, *our memories are useful when they remind us of God's
goodness, not our guilt.* This is the fruit of godly rather than worldly
sorrow.

God tells us to "forget the former things; do not dwell on the past"
(Is 43:18), *and* to "remember the former things, those of long ago; I
am God, and there is no other; I am God, and there is none like me"
(Is 46:9). God wants us to forget our sins and remember his greatness,
to disregard our sins and regard his grace. We are not to dwell on our
misdeeds but on the things he has done.

Now as I think about my past sin from college, I seek to remember
not so much my failure as God's forgiveness. "Amazing grace, how
sweet the sound that saved a wretch like me." I am learning the lesson
we all must learn: to focus more on his amazing grace and not just
on my wretchedness.

God's Offer

To focus on our sin without simultaneously acknowledging God's
forgiveness is to invite despair and defeat. To focus on God's wrath
and not his grace is to live a fearful rather than a free existence.
Because of God's grace, we receive something we don't deserve—his
love and forgiveness. Because of God's mercy, we don't receive what
we deserve—punishment for our sins. In his presence we feel both
sorrow at our guilt and joy at his grace. He knows that in and of
ourselves we can do nothing about the guilt and guilty nature that
have isolated us from fellowship with him. So he made a way for us
to be restored to right relationship with him.

God offers forgiveness to those who accept his gift of love through
Jesus Christ. He longs for us to fall on our knees, admitting our

guilt-ridden, sinful nature as well as our specific sins. As we receive the wondrous, undeserved gift of forgiveness, we are free from our past.

The story of the prodigal son illustrates God's immense and amazing love and forgiveness. After squandering his family inheritance on wild living, the son plans, "I will go . . . back to my father and say to him: Father, I have sinned against heaven and against you. I am no longer worthy to be called your son; make me like one of your hired men" (Lk 15:18-19). When the son returns his father could have said, "I forgive you for wasting the money and for living a shameful life. Yes, you may become one of my servants." Or he could have said, "Yes, I forgive you, but you don't need to stay in the servants' quarters; you can come live in the main house."

Instead, the father not only forgives the son but restores him to his original family position. "The father said to his servants, 'Quick! Bring the best robe and put it on him. Put a ring on his finger and sandals on his feet. Bring the fattened calf and kill it. Let's have a feast and celebrate. For this son of mine was dead and is alive again; he was lost and is found.' So they began to celebrate" (Lk 15:22-24).

The father not only forgave his son; he also restored and solidified his identity by giving him a welcome-home party, a ring and a robe, indicating his position and importance. Like the prodigal son, we aren't just forgiven; we are also given status as a member of God's family. He welcomes us with open arms when we return to ask him for forgiveness. He considers us worthy, valuable and lovable. His forgiveness erases our sin and establishes us as his beloved children.

A Spanish man and his teenage son weren't getting along. One day the son ran away from home. The father immediately began looking everywhere for him. Finally, in desperation, the father placed an ad in the newspaper in Madrid, the largest city in Spain. The ad read, "Dear Paco, meet me in front of the newspaper office at noon. All is forgiven. I love you. Your father." The next day at noon in front of the newspaper office there were eight hundred Pacos, all seeking forgiveness from their fathers.

Just like that father and his son, God is placing an ad, calling each of us by name, offering forgiveness.

Application Questions
   1. Which of the "assurances" do you find most comforting?
   2. Do you get stuck regretting past sins? What can you do to help get freed from them?
   3. Which of the obstacles to freedom get in the way of your fully appropriating God's forgiveness?

Prayer
Lord, thank you that you forgive us and that your gift of forgiveness is unconditional, continual and free. Amen.

SEVENTEEN

Winning
the
Battle

*E*ver had gum in your hair? A bat in your house? A disgusting odor in your kitchen? A pebble in your shoe? A bee trapped in your car? Ever held a hot potato?

I have had gum stuck in my hair—a very unpleasant ordeal. The remedy required a sacrifice of some locks of hair. When we had a disgusting odor in our kitchen, we invested in numerous air fresheners, opened all the doors and windows and cleaned out the refrigerator and wastebaskets. When a bee flew into our car, we immediately sought all means possible to rid ourselves of the stinging invader. It seemed that the kids' screams were louder and longer than ever before. The bee departed just before our nerves did.

When an unwanted intruder or situation faces us, we immediately seek ways to alleviate the problem. We don't hesitate; we are moved to swift action. We may have to make sacrifices, face hard work or draw upon our ingenuity, but we do it because we don't want to be burdened, hassled or inconvenienced.

This is how we should deal with bad guilt. We should view it as the gooey gum, the hot potato, the painful pebble in the shoe, the disgusting odor or the unwanted creature. Even though it may take effort, work and resourcefulness, we should immediately seek ways to rid ourselves of it.

Reviewing Our Strategies

In the past, our efforts may have incorrectly focused on ridding ourselves of all guilt. We have come to realize that only the excessive, unnecessary and unhealthy guilt needs to be eradicated. Good guilt is not the gum stuck in our hair but the brush that untangles the mess. It is not the pebble stuck in the shoe but the cushioned sole that makes life's journey easier.

Responses to Guilt			
Fight	Flee	Surrender to Guilt	Surrender to God
Develop defensive strategies and skills	Run, hide, escape—develop masks and disguises	Become enslaved to guilt, condemnation and self-punishment	Discern source of guilt; if false, ignore and evade; if true, respond with godly sorrow, conviction and confession, forgiveness and freedom
Belief: All guilt is bad, unwanted			Belief: Some guilt is bad, some good
Result: Distracts us from God			Result: Draws us to God

Our responses to guilt are the same responses we have when we are threatened—we fight, flee or surrender. When we believe that guilt is the enemy to be avoided, we become easily distracted from God as we continually seek ways to lessen the guilt we feel.

God's strategy is that we surrender *to him*. When we yield to him, we are better able to discern whether the source of guilt is or isn't from him. Good guilt draws us to God and helps clarify our need for his mercy and grace as we repent, confess and receive forgiveness.

The Healthy and Unhealthy Paths

Our goal is to have a heart that serves God and desires to follow his will. To surrender to God rather than to guilt, we must understand God's plan with regard to guilt.

The Unhealthy Path	The Healthy Path
Believe that guilt can and should be avoided	Acknowledge that guilt is inescapable
Remain unaware of our faulty battle plans and continue using them over and over	Become aware of our ineffective strategies to deal with guilt
Run and hide from guilt	Face and embrace guilt
Lump all guilt together and label it as unhealthy	Understand the sources of our guilt in order to develop better discernment
View guilt as either all bad (the dreaded enemy) or all true (from God)—extremes	Discern between good and bad guilt, between what is and isn't of God
Develop either an overly sensitive or extremely numb (blunted) heart and mind toward guilt	Develop a soft, humble heart and a listening ear to better receive the conviction of the Holy Spirit
Remain stuck in a cycle of denial or condemnation, untouched by good guilt's transforming power	Repent, confess and receive forgiveness for our true guilt; ignore false guilt

Our desire is to honor and glorify our Lord and Savior Jesus Christ, who has given us forgiveness and a means to eternal life. As we choose to follow the healthy way of dealing with guilt, we lessen the world's control over our lives and give God more control.

Getting at Guilt

Earlier we learned that the masks, disguises and defenses we use to protect us from guilt actually trap it inside (figure 2).

The layers represent the masks, disguises and defenses we use to protect ourselves from guilt. The further we get from the inner circle (our feelings and thoughts), the harder it is to get at guilt. These layers, meant to protect us from guilt, actually prevent us from dealing with it. In this sense, our defenses are like a heavy suit of armor that burdens and restricts us rather than protects us. We foolishly don't realize that it is actually the suit itself that must be shed.

But God has another plan. His love and forgiveness are the tools needed to break through and remove the guilt that is infecting our souls. His forgiveness removes the guilt of our sin, and his love drives out the fears that fuel our guilt (1 Jn 4:18). Whether we experience fear

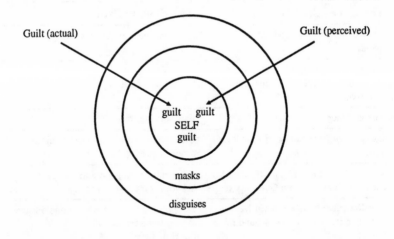

Figure 2: Guilt goes in and gets trapped inside.

of punishment, fear of failure or fear of abandonment and loneliness, God's love forces our fears to flee along with the feelings of guilt that accompany them (see figure 3).

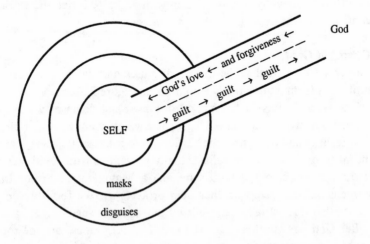

Figure 3: God breaks through our fortifications and façades, filling us with his love and forgiveness. He makes a way for our guilt to get out.

He is the only one who can successfully penetrate the walls we build. He not only breaks through our self-destructive methods but also gives us the strength to see ourselves without the masks and disguises we have used for so long. He reminds us of his love and tells us that we needn't be afraid of guilt any longer.

The Depths of Guilt and Despair

God's forgiveness reaches even to the depths of despair and guilt experienced by those of us whose true guilt reflects devastating and crushing deeds. We may feel responsible in one way or another for a tragedy—whether an accident, death, illness, abortion, suicide or injury. Or perhaps we have vandalized, stalked, abused, murdered, embezzled, had an affair or become addicted. Our guilt may seem unquenchable and uncontrollable. We may wonder if God's forgiveness can reach as low as we feel, if it can break through the many barriers and disguises we have used to insulate us.

God's forgiveness is all-sufficient and all-encompassing. It is able to penetrate any walls we build. If you feel your guilt is greater than his grace, or if guilt continues to plague you, seek professional or pastoral counseling. You may be unable to see your way through the maze and need an objective outsider to help guide you.

God's Sufficient Grace

However big our trespass, however rotten we feel, God's grace is able to rescue us from the depths of our sin and shame. In our moments or years of struggle, his grace is abundant and sufficient to see us through (Rom 5:17; 2 Cor 12:9). By his grace we also find hope and encouragement when we face adversity and trials. "Our Lord Jesus Christ himself and God our Father . . . loved us and by his grace gave us eternal encouragement and good hope" (2 Thess 2:16).

When we are overcome with temptations or memories of our sinful past, his grace continues to pour forth healing through the undeserved wonder of his forgiveness. "But where sin increased, grace increased all the more" (Rom 5:20). Remember, God is able to help us in *all* things at *all* times, giving us *all* that we need (2 Cor 9:8).

Winning Peace

Paul Hoffman once said, "We should wage war not to win war, but to win peace." We have waged war against bad guilt not just to defeat it but, more important, to gain that peace that passes all understanding (Phil 4:7). Because of Christ's shed blood on the cross, we are victorious. "This is the victory that has overcome the world . . . our faith. Who is it that overcomes the world? Only he who believes that Jesus is the Son of God" (1 Jn 5:4-5). Our victory is assured if we believe in the one who has the power to overcome the world. Only he offers true freedom from guilt. Paul Tournier summarizes, "A personal relationship with God . . . is the true solution to guilt."[1]

Let us echo the words written by Vicomte Turenne after the battle of Dunen in 1658: "The enemy came. He was beaten. I am tired. Good night."

Application Questions

1. Which response to guilt do you tend to use most—fight, flee or surrender? When and how do you respond in that way?

2. Do you sometimes feel that your guilt is "unquenchable and uncontrollable"? Do you wonder if God's forgiveness can reach as low as you feel? If so, have you considered receiving professional or pastoral counseling? What keeps you from seeking professional assistance? To whom would you go?

3. In order to "overcome the world," we must believe that "Jesus is the Son of God" (1 Jn 5:4-5). If you do not yet believe this, what is keeping you from doing so?

Prayer

Father, thank you for your victory over sin and death. Your grace is sufficient to cover the depths and despair of our guilt. Thank you for breaking through and making a way for our guilt to get out and for filling us with your love and forgiveness. Amen.

Notes

Chapter 1: Why Examine Guilt?

[1]C. S. Lewis, *The Screwtape Letters* (New York: Macmillan, 1959).

[2]Keith Krull, talk presented at First Baptist Church, Vancouver, B.C., October 1994.

[3]James Dobson, *Emotions: Can You Trust Them?* (Ventura, Calif.: Regal Books, 1980), p. 17.

[4]André Ravier, *A Do-It-at-Home Retreat: The Spiritual Exercises of St. Ignatius Loyola* (San Francisco: Ignatius, 1989), p. 231.

Chapter 2: Good Versus Bad Guilt

[1]Herbert Morris, "The Decline of Guilt," *Journal of Ethics*, October 1988, p. 76.

[2]Harlan J. Wechsler, *What's So Bad About Guilt?* (New York: Simon & Schuster, 1990), p. 17.

[3]Bruce Narramore and Bill Counts, *Freedom from Guilt* (Eugene, Ore.: Harvest House, 1974), p. 36.

[4]Don Richmond, "False Guilt: Escape to Grace," unpublished manuscript, May 1994.

[5]Judith Viorst, *Love and Guilt and the Meaning of Life, Etc.* (New York: Simon & Schuster, 1979), p. 23.

[6]Earl D. Wilson, *Counseling and Guilt: Resources for Christian Counseling* (Waco, Tex.: Word, 1987), p. 47.

[7]Dan Allender and Tremper Longman III, *Cry of the Soul* (Colorado Springs: NavPress, 1994), p. 172.

Chapter 3: Understanding Guilt
[1]Keith Krull, seminar presentation, First Baptist Church, Vancouver, B.C., Spring 1995.
[2]Malcolm A. Jeeves, in *Topical Encyclopedia of Living Quotations,* ed. Sherwood Eliot Wirt and Kersten Beckstrom (Minneapolis, Minn.: Bethany, 1982), p. 102.
[3]Narramore and Counts, *Freedom from Guilt*, p. 36.
[4]Dobson, *Emotions*, p. 26.
[5]Susan Miller, *The Shame Experience* (Mahwah, N.J.: L. Erlbaum Assoc., 1985), p. 47.
[6]Ty Colbert, *Why Do I Feel Guilty When I've Done Nothing Wrong?* (Nashville: Thomas Nelson, 1993), p. 21.

Chapter 4: The Happy Ending
[1]Don Cousins and Judson Poling, *Friendship with God* (Grand Rapids, Mich.: Willow Creek Resources/Zondervan, 1992), p. 26.
[2]Paul Tournier, *Guilt and Grace* (San Francisco: Harper & Row, 1962), p. 185.
[3]Charles R. Swindoll, *Grace Awakening* (Waco, Tex.: Word, 1990), p. 62.
[4]Ibid., p. 289.
[5]Tournier, *Guilt and Grace,* p. 160.
[6]Swindoll, *Grace Awakening*, p. 25.

Chapter 5: Guilt Attacks
[1]Joel Wells, *Coping in the Eighties: Eliminating Needless Stress and Guilt* (Chicago: Thomas Moore, 1986), p. 18.
[2]Donald E. Sloat, *The Dangers of Growing Up in a Christian Home* (Nashville: Thomas Nelson, 1986), pp. 92, 94.
[3]Lucy Freeman and Herbert S. Strean, *Guilt: Letting Go* (New York: John Wiley & Sons, 1986), p. 165.

Chapter 6: Family & Guilt
[1]Paula McDonald and Dick McDonald, *Guilt Free* (New York: Grosset & Dunlap, 1977), pp. 34-5.
[2]Dobson, *Emotions*, p. 34.
[3]Wynnae Huizinga Bliss, personal note, February 1995.

[4]McDonald and McDonald, *Guilt Free*, p. 46.

[5]Note: *toxic* is a term used by Susan Forward and Craig Buck to describe unhealthy guilt-producing behaviors. See their book *Toxic Parents* (New York: Bantam, 1989).

[6]Sloat, *Dangers of Growing Up in a Christian Home,* p. 86.

[7]Narramore and Counts, *Freedom from Guilt*, p. 23.

[8]Ibid., p. 25.

[9]General Lewis B. Hershey, news summaries, December 31, 1951.

[10]Sloat, *Dangers of Growing Up in a Christian Home,* pp. 213, 27.

[11]Patricia H. Rushford, *What Kids Need Most in a Mom* (Old Tappan, N.J.: Revell, 1986), pp. 20, 25, 26.

Chapter 7: Religion & Guilt

[1]McDonald and McDonald, *Guilt Free*, p. 48.

[2]Wechsler, *What's So Bad About Guilt?* pp. 30-31.

[3]Tournier, *Guilt and Grace*, p. 175.

[4]Sloat, *Dangers of Growing Up in a Christian Home,* p. 288.

[5]Hal Lindsey, *Satan Is Alive and Well on Planet Earth* (Grand Rapids, Mich.: Zondervan, 1972), p. 186.

[6]Paul Tournier, *A Place for You*, trans. Edwin Hudson (New York: Harper & Row, 1968), pp. 115-16, 128-29.

[7]Sloat, *Dangers of Growing Up in a Christian Home,* p. 105.

[8]Narramore and Counts, *Freedom from Guilt*, p. 113.

[9]Ibid., p. 112.

[10]Ibid., pp. 108-9.

Chapter 8: Expectations, Culture & Guilt

[1]Wilson, *Counseling and Guilt,* p. 64.

[2]Wells, *Coping in the Eighties,* p. 22.

[3]Georgia Witkin, *Passions: How to Manage Despair, Fear, Rage and Guilt and Heighten Your Capacity for Joy, Love, Hope and Awe* (New York: Villard/Random House, 1992), p. 96.

[4]McDonald and McDonald, *Guilt Free*, pp. 74, 67.

[5]Richard Foster, *Celebration of Discipline* (San Francisco: Harper & Row, 1978), p. 70.

[6]Pope John Paul II, *Crossing the Threshold of Hope* (New York: Random House, 1994), p. 165.

Chapter 9: Guilt-Ridden Masks

[1]John Drakeford, *Integrity Therapy* (Nashville: Broadman, 1950), p. 38.

[2]Ibid., p. 37.
[3]Frederick Buechner, *The Hungering Dark* (San Francisco: HarperCollins, 1985).

Chapter 10: Guilt-Driven Disguises
[1]Freeman and Strean, *Guilt: Letting Go*, p. 109.

Chapter 11: The All-Consuming Battle
[1]Tournier, *Guilt and Grace,* p. 175.
[2]Wechsler, *What's So Bad About Guilt?* p. 97.

Chapter 12: A Winning Strategy
[1]Richmond, "False Guilt."
[2]Tournier, *Guilt and Grace*, pp. 121-22.
[3]Mike Mason, "The Wizard of Uz," *Crux* (Regent College) 23 (June 1991): 36.

Chapter 13: Identifying the Enemy
[1]Wechsler, *What's So Bad About Guilt?* p. 74.

Chapter 14: Dealing with Bad Guilt
[1]Chip Ingram, sermon, Santa Cruz Bible Church, Santa Cruz, California, July 8, 1995.
[2]Dale Carnegie, *How to Win Friends and Influence People* (New York: Simon & Schuster, 1948), pp. 124-25.

Chapter 15: Conviction & Confession, Not Condemnation
[1]G. Walters, "Holy Spirit," in *The New Bible Dictionary*, ed. J. D. Douglas (Grand Rapids, Mich.: Eerdmans, 1962), pp. 533-34.
[2]Phillip Swihart, *How to Live with Your Feelings* (Downers Grove, Ill.: InterVarsity Press, 1976), p. 28.
[3]Wilson, *Counseling and Guilt,* p. 37.
[4]Wechsler, *What's So Bad About Guilt?* pp. 158, 143.
[5]B. B. Warfield, *Biblical and Theological Studies* (Grand Rapids, Mich.: Baker Book House, 1968), pp. 365-66.
[6]Fritz Laubach, "metamelomai," *The New International Dictionary of New Testament Theology,* ed. Colin Brown, 3 vols. (Grand Rapids, Mich.: Zondervan, 1975), 1:356.
[7]John Gilmore. "O. Hobart Mowrer: A Psychological and Theological Critique," in *Counseling and the Human Predicament: A Study of Sin, Guilt and*

Forgiveness, ed. LeRoy Aden and David Benner (Grand Rapids, Mich.: Baker Book House, 1989), p. 93.

[8]Dietrich Bonhoeffer, *Life Together* (San Francisco: Harper & Row, 1954), p. 113.

[9]Richmond, "False Guilt," pp. 5-6.

[10]Bonhoeffer, *Life Together*, p. 120.

[11]Ibid., pp. 114, 116.

[12]Foster, *Celebration of Discipline*, p. 129.

[13]Wilson, *Counseling and Guilt*, pp. 35-36.

Chapter 16: Forgiveness & Freedom

[1]Gilmore, "O. Hobart Mowrer," p. 93.

[2]Leon Morris, "1, 2 and 3 John," in *The New Bible Commentary: Revised,* ed. Donald Guthrie et al. (Downers Grove, Ill.: InterVarsity Press, 1970), p. 1262.

[3]Conversation with Lane Webster, University Baptist Church, Santa Cruz, California, February 1995.

[4]John White, *Putting the Soul Back in Psychology* (Downers Grove, Ill.: InterVarsity Press, 1987), pp. 33-36.

Chapter 17: Winning the Battle

[1]Tournier, *Guilt and Grace*, p. 167.